My Desert, My Gift

HOW OBEDIENCE CAN TRANSFORM A WILDERNESS SEASON INTO A BLESSING

Shawna Elizabeth

Shawna Elizabeth
07090 68th Street
South Haven, MI 49090
www.mydesertmygift.com

Book Layout ©2017 BookDesignTemplates.com

Ordering Information:
Quantity sales. Special discounts are available on quantity purchases by corporations, associations, and others. For details, contact the "Special Sales Department" at the address above.

My Desert, My Gift/ Shawna Elizabeth. —1st ed.
ISBN 9798669870188

Contents

Dedicated to the One who has walked with me through every season.

All along, let us remember, we are not asked to understand, but simply to obey.

—Amy Carmichael

Preface

Jesus once told a story about two brothers. It is not one of His more well-known stories. Basically, a dad was trying to get his sons to do their chores. When he went to tell the first son to work in the vineyard, the son said he didn't want to do it, but later he changed his mind and headed out to do what his father asked. The second son did the exact opposite. He told his father he would get the job done but got hooked on a video game or something and didn't show up to do the work.

Jesus asked the people which of the sons obeyed their father, and everyone agreed that it was the first son.

Once one of my leaders compared me to the first son. I think he meant it as a complement. I think he meant that I don't always know why God is asking something of me, that I tend to resist at first because I don't understand, but in the end I end up submitting and obeying.

He was right, but I wish I could be a different brother. A brother that just says yes and does whatever the father asks the moment he says it. I picture a willing servant who hops up and says "your wish is my command!" as soon as the father opens his mouth. But I have opinions about a lot of things, and sometimes I wonder if I missed my calling to become a lawyer. When something is being asked of me that I don't like or understand, I usually will not stay silent. I'll ask questions, maybe grumble a bit (hey, no one said you have to be a saint to write a book!) and maybe present a couple alternative options. But, in the end, I try to follow what I know God is asking of me. After all, who wants to be out of the will of God?!

Proverbs 16:1-2 in The Passion Translation says,

> *"Go ahead and make all the plans you want, but it's the Lord who will ultimately direct your steps. We are all in love with our own opinions, convinced they're correct. But the Lord is in the midst of us, testing and probing our every motive."*

Thanks to Adam and Eve's choice in the Garden of Eden, obeying God doesn't come naturally to any of us. Our Creator knows what is best for us and wants what is best for us, but so often we resist simply because we don't see how He sees and we think we know better. We chose our own plans, often ignoring Him altogether. However, if we simply turn our hearts to Him, inviting Him into our lives and seeking His will over our own, we have a chance of becoming the obedient children He created us to be. It is never easy, but it is possible.

I've been exercising regularly lately and that experience has just confirmed to me that I am 100% the first son. When my coach tells me what the workout will be, my typical response is "Ughhhh are you serious?! Is that even possible?" When he increases the weight I need to lift I say something like "Why??? I think it was heavy enough already." Anyways, I'm trying to work on speaking a little more positively in the gym, but after all the whining, I shut up and do it and it's never more than I can handle.

The thing is, our grumbling and resistance isn't honoring, but it also doesn't intimidate God. I think when we're throwing our little tantrums about what He is asking us to do He just stands back, laughs a bit, and waits it out. Kind of like we did with my four year old niece when she threw herself on the floor and said, "I can't move! My legs are bwoken!" We had to hold back our laughter at her dramatic scene, because of course her legs weren't broken at all. And that's what God does with us. He patiently waits for us to cut the drama, because He knows that we are perfectly capable of accomplishing what He's asking of us.

I think when we finally get over it and obey, it is even more pleasing to Him, because it costs us something. We have to lay down our own desires and what we think is right. We have to wrestle with our doubts and fears and pride until we're able to pull ourselves together and obey what He's asking of us.

This book is my story. It's a culmination of the many tantrums and times I've wrestled with God, the times I've missed it and the times I ended up right where I was supposed to be. It's a book about the simplest and hardest part of life: obedience, with all of its costs and all of its rewards.

After all, I didn't have any intention of ending up where I am now.

CHAPTER ONE

Living It Out

I was just a normal, if not pretty awkward, 14 year old when I went on my first mission trip to Guatemala. I was a little girl who always dreamt of travel and definitely didn't want to do anything normal with my life, so I was mostly excited for the adventure. The fact that it was a mission trip, and there would be hundreds of other people going, helped my parents to say yes to my insane request. I raised the money and off I went!

I don't entirely know what I was expecting to happen on this two week trip, but it changed my life. My eyes were opened to the boundless zeal other young people had for Christ, to the immense need of the world, and to the incredible abundance that I lived with. This was to be expected from one's first mission trip. What might not be expected was the conclusion I came to as a result. As I stood in front of my small home church and shared photos of myself with paint smeared on my face, holding poor little children, I was asked if I was going to go back to Guatemala again soon. I didn't have to think much before I responded, "No. I had a really good trip and God taught me a lot, but I don't ever plan on doing missions again. I think I'm called to America."

My itch for adventure had been temporarily scratched. I had helped some people, but that was the end of it as far as I was concerned. The thing is, that wasn't the end of what God had in mind.

I had always had an understanding of who God is, that He loved me, and I think in some ways I loved Him. But that trip started a season in my life of really getting to know what a relationship with Him looked like. He began to pursue me, or maybe He always was, and I only then started to reciprocate the pursuit. I started to encounter Him in real ways. I started going to a youth group that believed in the gifts of the Holy Spirit. The thing was, whenever I had powerful encounters with God in worship and prayer, I saw nations. I saw people from every tribe worshipping Him in colorful garments. I saw the faces of the lost before me, calling out to me, pulling me to do something. I would weep as I felt the burden and the love of the Father for these people, His children who were separated from Him.

While God was showing me nations, I was begging Him to speak to me about my future. It's pretty funny actually that I thought they were two separate topics. I was a junior in high school and it was time to start applying for colleges. If you've already been through that season you know it is one of the most stressful decisions a young person can make. I was just concerned about making it through the day without embarrassing myself by tripping in the hall or forgetting my locker combination; I didn't know what career I wanted to dive into, potentially for the rest of my life! I had only lived for 16 years and I had a limited amount of time to figure out what I wanted to do for the next 60! Or at least, that's what the pressure was telling me.

Since I was learning about God, the Holy Spirit, and His involvement in my life, I practiced fasting and seeking Him for direction. I was SO hungry to meet Him, to know Him more, and to know what He wanted for my life. Somehow, I knew that the only good place for me to be was where He wanted me.

Many people around me, including my parents and pastor, thought the medical field would be a good route for me and I latched onto that idea. It was kind of a win-win. I could help people and I could also be "normal" and live the American dream. I could even go for some quick trips to other nations and help people there. It was a huge bonus that I was good at math and science and didn't mind the idea of continuing to study for... well for many, many years. I started to pursue this idea more, researching schools that had good programs for pre-med, different branches of practicing medicine, and exactly how long I would have to study.

I landed on the idea of becoming a pediatric oncologist. I'm honestly not sure why I thought it was a good idea to pursue one of the most potentially depressing fields of medicine, but I do know that I never wanted to do anything "normal" or expected. I also wanted to bring transformation, although I don't think I consciously realized it at the time. I wanted to go to the saddest, sickest people to bring joy and healing.

However, I was learning that God's direction for my life would be much better than my own, so I kept waiting and pressing in to hear what He wanted.

One day, at the end of youth group, one of our leaders came up and began to pray over me. She said that during the sermon when someone read the verse that says, "Many are called but few are chosen," God instantly brought me to her mind.

Then she said, "You know what you are supposed to do, just say yes to Him." When she walked away I started to feel frustrated and angry with God because I felt like He was avoiding answering me directly. I had been telling Him over and over that I wanted to follow Him if He would just speak to me about what that looked like! But just a moment later, He spoke. I felt the words coming from inside of me more then I heard them through my ears. He said, "You're going to be a missionary."

I crumpled to the ground in that moment and wept. A very minuscule part of me was happy that He answered me, but a bigger part was overwhelmed by the call. I had been praying for months, "God whatever you want me to do, I'll do it, just tell me." And now He told me, but I didn't think I wanted to do it. I didn't know that obeying the call would mean *this*! I wanted to rewind and take back all the words I had said to God in the weeks and months before, all the prayers I had prayed during worship times, all the cries of devotion, because I knew that now I had to obey. I was the one who asked for the call; I couldn't say no now.

I was learning that obedience isn't just saying you will go anywhere or do anything, it's actually doing it. It's one thing to want to be obedient, it's another thing to actually be obedient. Like the second son in the parable I shared in the introduction to this book, intending to obey isn't obedience. I was challenged to decide: which son did I want to be?

Words are meaningless if they aren't paired with action. Promises are void if they aren't fulfilled. I'm sure God enjoys the sentiment of our words of devotion, but I think He appreciates when we live it out even more. We expect the people who mean the most in our lives to communicate honor and love through their actions, so what better way can we express those things to God except through our active obedience?

I'm not married or in a relationship, but I know that when couples are first falling in love they have a lot of sweet things to say to each other, vows of how they will take care of each other, spend their lives together, make memories and build a family. However, after time passes and responsibilities increase, those words don't carry as much weight as things like doing the dishes, remembering to pick up the kids from school, and remaining faithful during the hardest seasons. The sentiments are nice, but the actions are the meat behind the words.

We sing songs to God telling Him "I surrender all," "You're all I want," "I'll go anywhere," or "I just wanna be where you are." But then when He gives us direction we usually respond with "well you don't mean right *now*, right?" or "you couldn't possibly mean *there*, you'll have to give me at least five more confirmations and then I'll consider," or "I'll do that one day when I have my own ministry, but I don't know how to do it now." He never seems to get us at a convenient time when we have enough resources, confidence, or availability for Him.

God isn't uninvolved in our lives. He thought them out from beginning to end before we were even born. I can tell you from experience, that His plans are way better than anything I could dream up for myself! We get to live out these amazing plans He has if we will only choose to follow them. However, we miss out on His best when we hold out our best from Him.

We might know that God's plans for us are the best and we might want those plans for our lives, but what about when those plans look completely contrary to what we expected them to be? What if they don't seem suitable to our personality or our skill set or our desires? What if they aren't as interesting or as easy as the plans God gave someone else? What do we do when the storms of life come and threaten our obedience?

In many countries around the world today it is illegal to preach the gospel, and in some of those countries you can even receive severe persecution just for converting to Christianity. In some places people face persecution from family members and social pressures. We saw this in Thailand. Young people are open to Jesus and they want to know more, but Buddhism is so predominant in their culture that if they were ever to forsake it, it's as if they are forsaking their own family, heritage, and nation to accept a foreigner's God. They have to decide if they are willing to sever relationships and bring disappointment and dishonor to their families, for the sake of choosing Jesus.

Nepal is also a nation where persecution runs rampant. It is a tiny nation sandwiched between two much more powerful nations: China and India. Known for being the home of Mount Everest, it is a beautiful country, covered almost entirely by the Himalayan mountains. It is a place where the colors are vibrant, the sounds are loud, and the scents are pungent. The nation takes pride in it's Hindu roots, but they also have a strong Buddhist influence. When you visit, the warmth of the people will embrace you immediately. That's probably why Nepal easily captured my heart: the humble people and the grand mountains.

The first time I visited I went on a ten day trek in the Himalayas to visit unreached tribal villages and share the love of Jesus with them. I was pumped up for the radical adventure, but I can assure you, I had no idea what I was getting into. Although I was young and tried to exercise every now and then, I was in no physical shape to be climbing mountains for ten days straight. When we were just thirty minutes in I thought I surely wouldn't make it. I had to stop to catch my breath every 100 meters, the thin air never seeming to fill my lungs, sweat stinging my eyes. I humbly handed my backpack over to a 12 year old Nepali with no shoes on. What I thought would be a 10 day walk in the park, turned into a moment-by-moment battle to take the next step.

We were hiking with a Nepali pastor friend who has a children's home in an area just outside of Kathmandu. We were in an area where Simon, one of his children, was from. We planned to visit Simon's village and some of his relatives with him. They were from the Sherpa tribe, known for their trekking abilities and famous for guiding and helping trekkers reach the peak of Mount Everest. Now I know why. The region we were in was so remote that many young people had to walk one to two hours each way to go to school, usually with only flip-flops on their feet. In some places they had to wade through rivers and hike up steep inclines to get to class. They were raised to climb mountains.

We hiked for five days one way, staying in villages along the way. The first few villages were larger and more developed because they were along the route some trekkers take on their way to Everest. We even met some pastors and stayed in churches. But as we took smaller, less known trails up through the mountains, the villages became more remote. The weather up there was pretty cold and we didn't sweat a lot, which was good because there weren't any showers. There was a spigot in the middle of the village that everyone shared, including the cows and goats. I could have used it to bath if I wanted, but I would have to bath in my clothes, and I would probably become the village entertainment of the night (a white person not only visiting the village but bathing under their spigot!).

As we drew nearer to the last village on our journey, Simon's hometown, we stopped at someone's home for afternoon tea. She was a distant aunt or some relative of Simon's and she was fifty-five years old. We peeled off our packs and made ourselves at home. As she prepared the tea, our pastor friend told us about the last time he met her, about a year ago. He told us that she was experiencing back pain at that time and he had prayed for her. As we watched her making tea, we could see that her movements were labored and she was in pain again, so the pastor asked her how she was doing. She responded by explaining that her pain was completely gone when he prayed for her before, but exactly twenty-one days after he left, it returned.

This woman was a buddhist, like most of the other people that belonged to her tribe. Just as her entire community was buddhist, her whole family was as well. However, when I first met her I saw something different in her. I saw her for who she could become: a lamp set on a stand. I knew that if this woman accepted Christ, she would be a powerhouse for the Lord.

Our new friend's house was positioned at the end of a path leading up a small hill where a buddhist monastery sat at the other end. While we rested at her house, a buddhist monk actually passed through and drank tea with us. He also suffered from pain, but his was in his hands and feet. When we prayed for his healing his face changed. He was full of shock as he stood up, shifting from foot to foot. After realizing the pain was really gone, a smile brightened his face as he began to dance around the room.

We began to share the gospel there, telling the woman that she had already seen the power of God at work in her life and now it was time to respond. She knew in her heart that what we were sharing was true, and she told us she believed, but she didn't want to give her life to Jesus because of the effect it would have on her. She would become the only believer in her family, in her village, and possibly in that whole area. And it wasn't just about having friends or social connections, it was about survival. Since it took her hours and maybe days of walking to reach more developed villages and markets, she and her family survived by trading goods with neighbors who had farms and livestock. The village was family, they cared for each other. But if she did something that went against the grain, something that the rest of the village wouldn't agree with, they could simply stop trading with her. The monks and the witchdoctors in the area could speak curses over her or use their influence to turn others against her. For her, this decision wasn't just about making time to read The Bible or wearing a cross necklace, it was a decision that would completely transform the way she lived, make her every day chores a challenge, alienate her, and perhaps even jeopardize her life. She didn't know if she was ready to make that decision alone.

As we continued to drink tea and fellowship with her, and share the truth about Jesus, a young man, another family member who had been quietly listening and observing, spoke up. He wanted to accept Jesus into his heart and follow Him. Because of his bold and eager desire, the woman also decided to surrender her life to The Lord, along with three others. Among them was Simon, the boy from the children's home, and his big brother who was helping us as a porter. These boys had both heard the good news before but hadn't been able to make a decision to follow yet. I guess the bravery and raw belief of the few people in the village that day gave them the extra push they needed.

You could sense the joy and freedom in the atmosphere as we sang a simple Nepali chorus "Danyabad Yesu," "thank you Jesus!" They had just made a weighty decision but the atmosphere was light because they knew that the reward would be far greater than the cost! We couldn't help but celebrate with them, not just because they were saved that day, but because we served a God that was worthy of our entire lives! Their decision had reminded me of the value of the Gospel and the goodness of what Jesus did for me.

For people in these countries, you don't just talk about following Jesus, it's all or nothing. Not so long ago, becoming a missionary could potentially cost your entire life. Many of the early missionaries packed their belongings in their coffin as they loaded onto a ship to sail across the world. Most of us don't consider the cost as much when we say yes to Him, but He is just as worthy of our entire lives when we live in the American suburbs as He is when we live in a remote village of a persecuted country. We might be able to be saved and remain in our comfort zones, but we are missing out on the fullness of the Gospel. We become blind to the full value and weightiness that it carries when we hold back our worship from Him and fail to live our lives as a living sacrifice.

When I was in worship while I was a teenager, I would always sense the Lord asking me if He was really all I needed. It was a gentle invitation to make Him my everything. At that time I was showing horses and I was VERY competitive. I had been riding horses since I was four years old and started showing at the age of 6, the minimum age for registration. I loved riding, especially competing. I loved the nerves, the challenge, the pressure, and the rewards. I had to ride my horse almost every day, drive over an hour to work with my trainer, and go to shows nearly every weekend during the summer. It wasn't only a big time commitment but also a financial responsibility. The horse itself could cost as much as a car, not to mention the equipment, the new outfits every season, the cost for lessons or boarding, transportation, show fees, and all the food. So as I began to know God more and sense His calling on my life, I began to question what the purpose of it all was. Yet, so much had been invested, it seemed like a waste to stop right as I was in my "prime,"with a new horse, training to compete in the biggest national competition.

I would tell God I was willing to give Him everything, but would add "but please don't make me give up riding." I saw that it was holding me back, yet I didn't want to let it go. The truth is we all have something that threatens to hold us back from absolute surrender. Eventually, God made it easier for me and the desire I had to ride and show began to fade rapidly. Not long after I decided to sell him, my horse started to have health problems and I wasn't able to compete with him anymore. God saw my heart's desire was to follow Him and He gave me the grace and the strength I needed to walk out my obedience.

People often make comments to me like: "What you're doing is great, I wish I had the time to do something like that." Or, "It's good that you're serving God while you're young, you don't have the responsibilities that I have." Or, "God really made you for this, I could never do what you do." They believe that I'm able to do what I do because my circumstances are different from theirs, so I'm not hindered by the things that hinder them. The truth is, I gave up a lot to be here.

I didn't have to bring my own coffin to the mission field, but I've had to leave some dreams and desires behind, not sure if I would ever see them again. When all my friends were getting married and starting to have kids, I moved to a place where my chances of finding a godly husband were reduced significantly. When my family was enjoying fun baby and childhood memories with my 4 nephews and my niece, I was living off of the occasional message and FaceTime call. The last time I went home my two youngest nephews didn't recognize me. When I could have channeled my drive to learn and succeed at a successful career, I began to live off the support of church members and family friends. When I could have kept a paying ministry job in my own home church, I had to leave them for the unknown.

This isn't an invitation to a pity party, it's a wake-up call. There's a cost for putting action to the call of God on our lives. For everyone. We can't tell God we will give Him everything and not expect it to be hard. It will cost something and it will be difficult. But even though obeying has been challenging, I haven't regretted it one bit. There's really no better place to be then in His will. Worthy is the Lamb to receive the reward for His suffering! Worthy is Jesus to receive every single sacrifice and act of obedience I have to give.

No more "I'll obey when..." or, "I'll obey if..." or, "I'll obey, but..." It's time to ask ourselves if we're willing to do this thing FOR REAL. We need to decide if He is worth our obedience, even if it leads us through frustrating seasons, hard circumstances, or even intense suffering.

Are you ready to say "I'll obey" and actually do it? Are you ready to practice obedience no matter what the cost? Are you ready to be a true disciple and live out your devotion to God?

CHAPTER TWO

Detours

I lived in Thailand for over three years. I didn't want to go there the first time, when I went for only ten weeks of training. After the training I went back to America for 10 months to raise funds and prepare to return to Thailand for two more years, but still it wasn't where I wanted to be. I didn't expect that I would stay in Thailand until even the thought of leaving would bring me to tears.

My call to Thailand began when I was about to graduate from studying global missions at Bible school. For the last semester, students studying missions were supposed to choose an internship to get some experience "out in the world". However, I was a 20 year old with "*lots of experience*" already and I already knew exactly where I was going and what I was going to do with my life. I knew that God had put the nation of Nepal on my heart and I was on a one-track mission to make that happen. Once I've set my mind on doing something I just go for it. I didn't want the distraction of an internship in a random country that didn't seem to have any benefit to get me where I was going. Those trips were supposed to be for people with no experience and no direction.

Instead of doing the internship, I was planning to continue to study another subject at the Bible school for my last semester, which I thought would be more beneficial for my future. This sounded like a brilliant idea to me at the time, a good use of time and money, and I would be holding my certificate before I knew it.

Well my plan was turned upside down one morning when I overslept. You know it's going to be a rough day when you sleep through multiple alarms. I woke up too late to go to chapel, so instead I went straight to my class. That day, chapel went late so I ended up arriving in the classroom a few minutes before everyone else. It was just me and my missions professor. When I arrived he said, "Shawna, just the person I've been meaning to talk to!" *Great. Did he know I skipped chapel that morning?* I felt like I was about to be in the hot seat but I had no idea what for.

"I was just wondering why you weren't planning on doing an internship next semester?"

Ahhhh. That's all. Well that was an easy explanation that I'd already given about a hundred times. I began to give him the speech I had given everyone else but suddenly my words sounded like a bunch of empty thoughts and excuses. My reasons didn't make sense as they came out of my mouth and eventually I just stopped trying to explain.

After I quit rambling and eating my own words my professor graciously just said, "Ok, but I really think you should consider doing an internship. I specifically think Thailand would be a good fit for you. Just promise me you'll pray about it."

I didn't have anything sensible to say so I just assured him that I would pray and then kept my mouth shut. That does not happen often so I must have been really dumbfounded.

The rest of the day I couldn't concentrate in class. I had this anxious feeling and my mind kept going back to the conversation from that morning. I couldn't change all my plans at that point! It was already much too late in the game! I already told everyone exactly what I would be doing for the next year and a trip to Thailand was NOT a part of that. I already knew where I wanted to go and what I wanted to do, so there was no reason to go to Thailand. Besides, everyone else had already submitted their applications for the internships. I would be late to apply and I NEVER do anything late.

Yet, I knew all these thoughts were coming because God was redirecting me. I knew that the anxious feeling was because all my plans were about to be thrown out the window, and I liked my plans. They were secure and led me directly to the destination where I was "sure" God wanted me as soon as possible.

After class I went home and opened up my Bible to read for a few minutes before work. The passage I was reading that day was 2 Corinthians 1, "Paul's Change of Plans." Verses 17-19 spoke directly to my pride and my lack of flexibility:

> *"Was I fickle when I intended to do this? Or do I make my plans in a worldly manner so that in the same breath I say both 'Yes, yes' and 'No, no'?*
>
> *But as surely as God is faithful, our message to you is not 'Yes' and 'No.' For the Son of God, Jesus Christ, who was preached among you by us—by me and Silas and Timothy—was not 'Yes' and 'No,' but in him it has always been 'Yes.'"*

God challenged me in that moment to always say an enthusiastic "yes" to Him, even when it means I need to say no to people or change my plans. He showed me that being flexible is not being fickle or wishy-washy as long as it is in complete obedience to Him.

I said yes that day to God's plan for me in Thailand, even though it didn't make sense in my narrow mind's imagination.

Sometimes we think we know the plan that's best for us, and our plans are probably really great! They probably make sense and they might actually get us to the right destination eventually. But God's plans are so much better. They might not be as direct or as sensible but His plans encompass more than we could imagine or plan for ourselves.

One of my favorite quotes is by Jim Collins. He says simply, "Good is the enemy of great." Often we allow our good plans, our good lives, our good season, to keep us from the fullness of what our Good Father in heaven has for us.

Just because God told us to do something, it doesn't mean that is all that He has for us. And a singular instruction He has given us is surely not the ultimate destination He has planned. He's not trying to get us to fulfill one big prophecy over our lives so that we can "arrive" at His purpose. Total obedience is the destination. He's trying to teach us to walk with Him wherever, whenever, and with whoever He's calling us to. There's probably a lot of other stuff He has for us along the path to fulfilling the promise, but if we're not willing to face a little change of plans we could completely miss it.

Of course, God was getting me into something bigger than I realized at the time. He wasn't just trying to get me to go to Thailand for ten weeks, but He was wanting to provide something for me that I didn't even realize I needed at the time: spiritual family.

Since I started college I had been helping one of my friends establish a non-profit organization working primarily in Nepal. She is a visionary, a dreamer, and I am a "let's get it done" kind of person, a doer. We had some other young friends on board with us, all of us barely twenty years old, and all excited for what God would do.

It was fun to be starting something from scratch, something new and fresh that we could call our own, and I was fully invested. The people I was working with were passionate, creative, and loved Jesus. It was all a part of the plan. I could go to Nepal whenever I wanted and have the backing of this new organization that I had helped set up. I knew I would be pioneering and it would be hard, but I was ready for the adventure! That is why, when I went to do the internship in Thailand, I wasn't necessarily interested or looking into being a part of a missions sending organization.

Go To Nations (GTN) was the organization conducting the training. They have sent hundreds of missionaries to over a hundred nations and have trained thousands of national ministers through their Bible Schools in the past 40 years. Basically, GTN is a spiritual family that is committed to raising up people to fulfill the Great Commission (found in Matthew 28:16-20). I didn't know any of this prior to joining the internship, but as I worked with them each week I felt that stirring and unsettling feeling inside, telling me that God was about to do something.

I was so strongly impacted by the leadership in Thailand during my internship. I could tell that they really believed I was worth investing in. They saw something inside of me and wanted to pull it out. I knew that this organization was bigger than anything that I have ever been a part of, and that they were a multi-generational spiritual family, something that I had been longing for. I knew I would need spiritual fathers and mothers to lead me in my calling, as well as brothers and sisters to walk beside me along the way.

Each week of the internship I would tell my mentor, "I don't know what I'm supposed to do!" I felt this warring in my heart, the same feeling I had the day the Lord was telling me to sign up for the internship. Deep down, I knew what I had to do, but I didn't want to do it. I knew that if I joined Go To Nations as a long-term missionary I would be coming under a greater spiritual covering and I would be submitted to their authority to speak direction into my life. I would also be required to do a two year apprenticeship in one of three countries. Nepal wasn't included on that list. I didn't want my ten week detour to turn into a two year distraction. Boxed in by my plan, it almost seemed easier to ignore the tugging of the Holy Spirit and just finish what I started.

Finally, around week nine, one of the regional directors of GTN came to teach us about leadership. One day he said to me "Shawna, you have something we need and we have something you need." That impacted me immensely because I knew he was right. I knew the organization would fill the gaps in my life and ministry that needed to be filled, and I knew that it would help me to develop my own gifts.

So again, I said a painful and reluctant *yes* to the redirection of the Holy Spirit. Again, He asked me to break down the protective walls I had built around my own plans and aspirations and allow Him to expand them.

We often invite God to direct us, but what we really want Him to do is affirm us. We say that we will go anywhere with Him, but the fine print of our hearts is specifying that, by anywhere, we really mean "any one of the top three choices that I've already chosen for myself." We limit God to our own wisdom and human knowledge of what's best for us and we expect Him to bless us in our lack of faith.

Other times, God has given us a target to shoot for, a promise over our lives, and we take it and run with it. We think that God needs help figuring out how to fulfill His destiny for our lives, so we idolize the promise and make our mission to achieve that goal more important than obeying the next step that God has for us. What started off as obedience to Him turns into striving and self-promotion.

The thing is, we can keep making our own plans and asking God to bless them, forcing Him to radically step in if He wants anything different, or we can fully surrender to God from the start and continue to live in surrender every step of the way.

Once, I was leading a team to Nepal and one of my contacts there decided to bring us to an unreached village on the border of Tibet where he had been a few times. We hired a jeep to take us up through the Himalayas, driving for hours. Driving in Nepal is always an adventure in itself. The driver has to beep the horn around each curve to make sure there are no cars coming from the other direction because the road is only wide enough for one and usually there is a steep cliff dropping off to one side. If there is another car coming, one of the vehicles will drive as close to the edge as possible and stop so the other one can squeeze by. During the rainy season there are a lot more stops, allowing you to get out and stretch your legs while vehicles are being pushed out of the mud. I have experienced a broken axle on a bus once and many blown tires. Not to mention the little streams that are driven through, the narrow bridges crossed, and a few extra passengers bumping around on the roof. All that to say, it had been a long day on the road.

Finally, we arrived in a village and the jeep driver said that it was the end of the line for him, he wouldn't drive us any further. The problem was, this wasn't the village we wanted to be in. We would have to drive for twenty more minutes or walk for a couple hours to get there. The driver said he would bring us the rest of the way for 2,000 rupees (about twenty dollars) or we could wait there in the village for the public bus that *might* show up in an hour or so. I was the leader so I had to make a quick decision. Transportation costs add up quite a lot when you are traveling with a team and our budget wasn't exactly abundant. Plus, I felt that this man was trying to rip us off, and I DO NOT like to be taken advantage of. I decided that we would take our chances and sit in the village to wait for the bus to come.

We went to a little convenient store cafe to sit and wait. We were a bit hungry and hot from all the travel and we noticed that the store had Coke and Oreos. We were so excited! When you are hours away from modern civilization, even if you don't normally consume junk food, Coke and Oreos become a glimmer of hope and familiarity. We treated the pastors who were traveling with us and we all enjoyed a tasty snack.

We also began to chat with the owner of the shop. He was a trekking guide and he owned a hotel so his English was pretty good. As we talked with him he shared a lot about his life and we eventually found out that he had two wives, one in Nepal and one in India. We simply listened to him, shared the gospel with him, and prayed for him. But he was quite closed and uninterested in what we had to say.

Two hours or more passed and it was already evening, but the bus still hadn't come. I had this sinking feeling in my stomach that I had made the wrong decision. Not only were we stuck sharing with a man who didn't seem to care, it was already too late to start walking to the next village. Plus we had ended up spending about twenty dollars on snacks anyways! We should have just paid the jeep.

I'm so thankful I had lighthearted team members. They got out the guitar we brought and started to play on the side of the road, making up random songs about our traveling experiences. After a few minutes there were a handful of kids standing at a distance watching us and our Nepali friends had an idea. They told us to prepare a skit and they would gather children and adults from the village to come see it. We threw something together in five to ten minutes and chose someone on our team to share their testimony. About twenty villagers came and heard the gospel, probably for the first time ever, and several of them even responded as we prayed a prayer of acceptance.

You know what happened right in the middle of our prayer? Our bus drove by! One of the other Nepalis chased it down and had them wait while we finished our little program. Then we grabbed all our stuff and climbed up on the roof of the bus!

The decision I made that day might have had the wrong motivation. It may not have been a great decision based on human wisdom, as it took longer and cost more to get to our destination, but God had a different purpose than saving time and money. His goal wasn't to reach the border village as efficiently as possible. He was thinking about hearts and lives, not just of those that heard the gospel, but ours as well.

Sometimes the routes God is leading us on feel like detours. Often it seems like we are going in a direction completely contrary to where we are supposed to be. Maybe we feel like we are delayed in going where He really wants us. In those times we need to trust that God is doing something in the journey; He's not just waiting for us to reach the destination. We can end up in the place that God told us to go, yet completely miss the way that He called us to get there. But if we always remember that the destination is obedience to Him, not to our plans, then we are already in the right place.

CHAPTER THREE

Death By Comparison

I didn't always want to live overseas and spread the love of Jesus. Sure, the lure of adventure always seemed to be calling my name, but Asia seemed foreign and strange to me. As a young girl I dreamt of exploring Europe, Hawaii, *maybe* South America, but not Asia.

Some people seem to think that in order to do missions you have to have something special in your DNA, gearing you to jump on a plane and help people. People often make comments to me revealing their belief that there's some natural trait specific to me that makes it easier and perhaps even more pleasurable to live on the exact opposite side of the world from family and friends, to constantly be out of my comfort zone, to abandon dreams and personal achievements, and to not be afraid of the future or the unknown. Maybe they're partially right, because

God definitely prepared me for this, but as far as I know my DNA doesn't look that different from everyone else's. I didn't necessarily dream of doing this from childhood, and it hasn't been an easy journey.

However, not everyone who makes this suggestion to me says it in the same way. Some reveal in their tone that they think I'm some sort of a freak of nature for not caring about the things "normal" people care about, or for not working a "normal" job to take care of myself. Other people make me feel like a superhero, able to accomplish things that others can't without any extra effort. I know these people mean well, but I can't help but wonder if their skewed perspective of me is really hindering them. Let me explain.

One of my leaders always said, "Comparison can only have two outcomes in your life: pride or insecurity." What he meant was that if we think others are somehow more special than us, then we will become ashamed of who we are; but if we think that others are somehow less than us, then we will become proud. Both of these emotions, pride and insecurity, can keep us from walking in what God has for us in our own lives.

"The source of revelation-knowledge is found as you fall down in surrender before the Lord. Don't expect to see Shekinah glory until the Lord sees your sin-

cere humility. Go ahead and make all the plans you want, but it's the Lord who will ultimately direct your steps. We are all in love with our own opinions, convinced they're correct. But the Lord is in the midst of us, testing and probing our every motive. Before you do anything, put your trust totally in God and not in yourself. Then every plan you make will succeed" (Proverbs 15:33-16:3 TPT).

Pride can keep us from fulfilling what God has called us to do. Often we get caught up in doing what "feels right" and we think that's the same thing as following the will of God. We might be doing something "better" than someone else, but winning an unspoken competition isn't an indication of obedience, and it can actually be a distraction. It becomes dangerous when we begin to think we have life figured out, when we think we know what's best for us, and we think what's best for us must be best for everyone else. Pride in what we do or where we are going can distract us from being willing to ask God what route He intends for us to take. Pride in our independence can keep us from seeing that we might be wrong or from asking for counsel. We might think we've got it made, but what does God think? Are we willing to stop and ask Him?

In the same way, insecurity and shame can keep us from our destiny too. When we believe that everyone else was dealt a better hand than us and we are not deserving of a good future, we will never pursue one. If we are continually limiting ourselves because we don't "feel" special, we will forever just go with the crowd. Shame cripples us from stepping out because it tells us that we are not good enough for success. The thing is, sometimes our shame is comfortable. It allows us to never face our fears as we leave the heroism to braver, more worthy people.

I recently watched *Crazy Rich Asians* for the second time. If you haven't seen it, I highly recommend it. The first time I watched it, I had so many deep thoughts and different perspectives on cross-cultural experiences and could actually relate in some ways since I live in an Asian context. This time however, I was reflecting a lot on shame and how it affects our ability to be present in our own lives as well as a part of society.

Here is a quick snapshot of the plot: Rachel is a Chinese American living in New York and she's dating a Chinese Singaporean, Nick, who brings her back to Singapore for a friend's wedding. Well, turns out his family is filthy rich, owns much of the nation's real estate, and is a part of the society's elite. Everyone knows who they are and they represent their culture as well as the highest fashion, morals, and standards. Needless to say, Rachel, raised by a single mom and immigrant in New York, didn't quite fit the family's expectations. She had no idea what she was getting into.

In one striking scene, Nick's mother encounters Rachel on the grand staircase of their enormous mansion. It looks like she's attempting to connect to Rachel as she tells her about how her own mother-in-law never approved of her, how she was never good enough for the family, and how hard it was for her to live up to the family's standards for many years. But then she says, "But having been through it all, I know this much: You will never be enough." Her point being: if I wasn't good enough, you definitely aren't.

After that encounter Rachel wanted to go hide under a rock, like I'm sure I would. She considered not even attending the wedding that they had flown all the way to Singapore to go to. One person's attack on her identity and her abilities led to shame, which tempted her to cower in a corner instead of taking her rightful place. Good thing she had a friend who helped her to see the truth of who she was and empowered her to see that the best way to conquer her enemy was to respond with confidence.

Our enemy will do everything that he can to keep us from realizing the power in our confidence. He'll cut us down until we think we're not enough to be who God meant us to be. Or he'll puff us up until we're convinced that we're already the hero of our story and there's nothing more to be done. Both tactics cripple us from using our authority and walking in the purposes God has for us.

Yet, true confidence tells us that we are enough because of Him. True confidence tells us that if He is telling us to do it, then He will give us everything we need. True confidence stands on the Word of God, not our own achievements or short fallings, to see His promises come to pass.

We need to be obedient to HIM, and that requires us to shut up the voice of the enemy when he tries to get us to focus on comparing ourselves to those around us and their callings. We need to walk in what God has given US to walk in and not what He's given someone else to walk in. Comparing ourselves to what works for someone else will only bring us to shame or pride.

Each of us have a role that we were created to play in the Kingdom of God, something we were created for. And each of us have an enemy who will do whatever he can to keep us from being who we are made to be. When we are missing in action from our role or our season because we want to be someone or somewhere else, we rob ourselves of growth and we cripple the body of Christ. It's only when we stop comparing our gifts, our calling, or our process to our brothers' and sisters' that we can walk in full obedience to God's plan.

CHAPTER FOUR

Own Your Season

"You [are able to] grow when you become content 'here and now', more than you are frustrated about not being 'then and there.'" Christine Caine

Comparison doesn't have to just be with other people. Sometimes we compare what we are doing now to what we experienced in the past or what we hope to experience in the future. This can be just as crippling because it keeps us from being responsible for our present obedience.

Being present where we are can be so much harder than it seems it should be. You would think it would be easy to see the things right in front of your face, to enjoy the moment you are in, to go deep with the people around you, but it's actually a great challenge for many of us.

This might come back to personality in some ways, but my mind tends to jump to the future more than remaining in the present. It can be difficult to recognize that the present is where God wants you to be when He's spoken things to you about the future. I can get in the mindset that the present is just a time that I pass through in order to arrive where I'm supposed to be. I shouldn't get too attached to the present because it won't last.

I wonder if this is why God doesn't show us our future as much as we want Him to. He wants us to chill and value where we are just as much as where we're going. The crazy thing is, yesterday, today was our future. And pretty soon our future will be our present! We never truly arrive in our future but we always live in our present. Yet, how much focus do we put on making ourselves at home in the here and now?

When I first moved to Thailand, I wrote a blog post about marrying the land. I wrote about making a conscious choice to invest myself in that land, to love the people, learn the language, and allow my heart to be there and not just pass through. Little did I know what that would actually look or feel like, or how long it would take. I thought I was invested and all in from the beginning, but now, looking back, I realize how far I came. A marriage relationship doesn't just happen instantly, it's built. It grows with time. Just in my last six months in Thailand I began to see the attachment and realize how much it would hurt to say goodbye. I didn't always feel that way, but it came after endless decisions to commit more, to love the people, to live in the moment.

In that blog post I talked about emotional commitment, never giving up on loving even when it gets hard. I had no idea what that would look like. I didn't know that I would mourn with two of our Thai students who each lost a parent when they were still young, and tell other countless students that they were still loved even though one (or both) of their parents had left them. I couldn't foresee that I would see one of our only disciples put in prison for a foolish, impulsive decision that was made out of pure motives, leaving us to care for his fourteen-year-old son, who repeatedly stole from us and eventually ran away. I didn't know that some of our most dedicated students would move to other cities after we had spent countless hours praying for and connecting with their families.

I had answered my door many mornings to my middle-aged Thai friend, struggling with her newfound faith, fearing she would never find another job after leaving her work at the bars. My phone would wake me up at midnight when she was heartbroken, fearing her boyfriend was cheating on her again. I reminded her that she didn't need to receive blessings from idols or ancestors when we walked by the statues and she started to bow her head. I urged her time and time again to open her heart for God to heal her, to release forgiveness and receive healing, to no avail.

I loved and I lost. I hoped and I was disappointed. I invested and, at times, received no return on my investment.

But here's the thing, I loved. I hoped. I invested. That, in itself, has been the greatest gift. When I wanted to move to an "easier" ministry, I stuck with it. And if I hadn't, I wouldn't have the family, the friends, the memories, the growth that I had.

Many of us want to have successful businesses or ministries, healthy families or friendships, strong spiritual walks or self-images, but we won't get to those places tomorrow if we aren't investing in them today. We can't arrive at having a flourishing, supernatural walk with God if we aren't willing to obey Him in the little things now. These things aren't usually born overnight, but take time, walking in faith and obedience.

When we look back we may see that we haven't taken as many steps forward as we would like, or maybe we've even taken some steps backwards, and we become discouraged. Sometimes our future destination can feel so unreachable, so far away. When we begin to think like this we aren't seeing how the things we are experiencing today are molding us.

In order to be a professional musician and play in front of a crowd you need to sit in a practice room by yourself and play the same song thousands of times. You need to play for thousands of hours when there is absolutely no one listening before you can have an audience. And I'm sure in that time of practicing, any future musician will have the thought that they will never make it out of that room. They will forever be stuck in musical limbo playing for an audience of one and never see their dreams fulfilled. Until one day the time comes and they become an "overnight success." The sudden success wasn't really sudden, it took years of preparation that no one saw.

One of my professors in Bible school gave the illustration of a hammer hitting a rock. If you are trying to break the rock it might take, for example, twenty-three hits with the hammer. On the first strike you see absolutely nothing. On the second strike, nothing. The third, the fourth, the fifth, all the same. Even until the twentieth strike, nothing happens, but on the twenty-first hit the rock gets a small crack. Imagine if you had given up on the 20th hit, sure that you were making no progress, and the rock could not be broken?

Often we don't see how what we are doing now will lead us to our future. When God called me to move to Thailand I felt like I was going in the opposite direction of where I was supposed to be. I felt like I had taken two steps forward and now He was asking me to take five steps back. If we begin to make decisions based on where we think we should be or where we want to go, we begin to move into striving to attain the promises of God, rather than trusting and getting there His way.

Striving to attain God's promises can have very bad fruit, we see it in the Bible. Abram had a promise from God that He would be the father of a multitude of descendants that couldn't even be numbered! Yet, year after year passed and the promise seemed to get more and more impossible. God kept speaking to Abram about the promise but nothing was happening, and Abe wasn't getting any younger. That's when he decided to take things into his own hands. He and Sarai decided that Abram should try to have kids with Sarai's servant instead. And that's exactly what he did. Except this wasn't the fulfillment of the promise that God had planned, this was merely a diversion. Abram begged God to accept Ishmael, the son born to Sarai's servant, as the heir but God wouldn't have it. God doesn't really do shortcuts.

Abe's Plan B brought bitterness and division to his family and birthed a whole other nation. The good news is that God blessed the Ishmaelites as well, because He brings good even out of our mistakes. But in the next chapter of Genesis (Genesis 17) we see God gives Abram a new name, Abraham, and Sarai becomes Sarah. God reminds them of the promise and at this point, Abraham laughs at Him! I can imagine what he's thinking: "I've waited all these years and haven't moved any closer to the promise, I even tried to take some action steps and that didn't work out either. I'm no closer to the promise then I was 24 years ago when it was given." He didn't realize though, that everything was about to change; his promised child came the next year.

There's a purpose in what you're going through now. There's something God is trying to do in your present that is preparing you and building you for your future. Don't rush it. Don't wish you were somewhere else. Don't try to produce the promise before it's due time. Don't wish to rewind or fast-forward time just because you don't understand where you are now.

What is God asking of you right now? What season has He placed you in? Are you really embracing it or are you waiting for your next big break? Whether you see it or not, your obedi-

ence to your season today will lead to the fulfillment of your promise tomorrow.

Don't spend your life wishing you were in another place or another position. Don't get so
caught up in the there and then that you fail to
be faithful in the here and now that God has
placed you in. The promise will come soon
enough. God will take care of that. It's up to us to
focus on the instructions He's given for this
present time and obey them. Keep chipping away
at the rock. Keep loving the person in front of
you. Keep believing in the midst of your waiting.

CHAPTER FIVE

Where to Put Expectations

Those of us who have lived at all have wrestled with expectations. I'm only twenty-five but I've already had my share of matches with expectations. Sometimes I end up pinned to the mat of defeat and disappointment, but other times I get to claim the victory. Expectations can be a tricky thing. You can't live with 'em, but you can't live without 'em.

With no expectations we have no dreams, no aspirations, and therefore no hope for the future. With no expectations we will never aim towards anything or try anything new. Expectation pushes us to seek after more. It encourages us to pray for something impossible to happen. It gives us motivation to keep showing up at our jobs even when they seem mundane. The hope that we will succeed or accomplish something causes us to make to-do lists and dream boards. It motivates us to show up for relationships because we expect people will be there for us.

However, our expectations can also sting us. We can put so much trust and faith in our expectations that when they are unmet we find ourselves devastated. Like the proverb says, "Hope deferred makes the heart sick." (Proverbs 13:12a, ESV) We risk a heart-sickness called disappointment when we put ourselves on the line to expect something. So we numb ourselves to stop expectation. Out of our disappointment we teach our children not to live with their heads in the clouds, not to shoot so high. We tell ourselves that healing isn't for today. We settle for a relationship with the next eligible bachelor that comes along. We convince our minds that God isn't invested in our daily lives and doesn't care about our minuscule expectations so we need to only shoot for humanly possible or controllable things. We begin to guard our hearts' affections not just from idols but from faith too, building a wall around our heart that will shield us from all external threats, including those made to spark hope and faith and dreams.

By trying to block out the disappointment we block out the hope too. Brené Brown has researched this concept and says it so well, "We cannot selectively numb emotion. If we numb the dark, we numb the light. If we take the edge off pain and discomfort we are, by default, taking the edge off joy, love, belonging, and the other emotions that give meaning to our lives."

As Christians, doing this often makes us feel or look more spiritual. We think that numbing ourselves to expectations is the same as surrendering our desires to God's will. We think that we are denying our own desires for what He wants. The truth is, we're not really surrendering our expectations when we deny ourselves the ability to even have them. We are stripping obedience of any sacrifice and we are emptying ourselves from having to surrender our true desires because apparently our hearts don't long for anything anyways. God doesn't call us to live a numb life void of desire. Instead He asks us to make *Him* the desire of our hearts.

I'm going to get a bit personal here because expectations are often quite personal. Being real about our desires can feel like we are exposing an intimate part of our heart. It's hard to be honest about what we truly want. It's much easier to just pretend we are above all of those weak feelings and just roll with the punches of whatever life brings at us.

I'm twenty-five years old and honestly, I expected to be married by now. The large majority of my friends are married and many of them have started families. One expectation that I had was that before I moved to Nepal, I would be married. I didn't want to go to Nepal alone, and I figured, surely God didn't want that either. Every time I pictured myself starting a life in Nepal I pictured the man of my dreams going with me. Of course, he would also have a burning passion for that nation and together we would take it by storm! But here I am in Nepal still very, very single.

What do we do with these expectations? In one of her teachings, Abi Stumvoll says, "Emotions are like kids, you can't put them in the trunk of your car but you can't let them drive either." I think that our expectations are the same way. We can't ignore them, convince ourselves we don't have them, or shut them down completely. But we also can't expect life to go as we expect it to 100% of the time.

The first thing we should do with expectations, is share them with the Father. Instead of hiding what we want because we fear He'll change it all anyways, or instead of pretending we are so surrendered to Him that we don't have our own desires, we should let Him in on those intimate parts of our heart.

Recently, I was reading Psalm 139. In the beginning David is making a declaration about how well the intimate God of the universe knows him and sees him. He writes,

"Lord, you know everything there is to know about me. You perceive every movement of my heart and soul, and you understand my every thought before it even enters my mind" (Psalm 139:1-2, TPT).

He continues to express how God created him and is always with him. But then, in the very end, this is what he says:

"God, I invite your searching gaze into my heart. Examine me through and through; find out everything that may be hidden within me. Put me to the test and sift through all my anxious cares" (Psalm 139:23, TPT).

Why would David make a point to say that God already knows everything there is to know about him, but then still feel the need to invite God to know him more? As I thought about it I realized: there's a difference between vulnerability and intimacy. Vulnerability isn't always voluntary. Cities can be vulnerable to attack, people can be vulnerable to sickness, sensitive information can be vulnerable to hackers. Vulnerability is exposure, being seen, and that can be a very positive thing, but it can also be used against you. Just because someone can see you, it doesn't mean you have a relationship with them. Just because God knew everything about David, it didn't mean they automatically had an intimate relationship. You can have vulnerability without intimacy but you can't have intimacy without vulnerability.

Intimacy is vulnerability that comes with an invitation. David wasn't just vulnerable to God, he invited the Father into his vulnerability, and that's what turned it into intimacy. God might know what we want, and He might know what He's going to do, but He wants to be invited into our expectations. We need to be open to inviting Him into our desires, wants, dreams, and motivations. Don't just invite Him into your house and make Him sit on the couch and watch while you try to fix up the mess. Invite Him to get His hands dirty with you and be a part of it. Stop holding Him at arms length as if He can't handle what's inside your heart. I know it's scary. He'll probably move some stuff around, and even throw away some things you want to hold onto, but it's so much better to have Him sort through our desires and show us what to do with them before they lead to the kind of hope deferred that will make our hearts sick.

That leads me to the second thing we should do with our expectations: surrender them to Him and allow Him to give us His desires.

There was a season when I really liked a guy. He was good looking, loved the Lord, and was full of passion and vision. There were some things that just didn't line up, I knew the timing wasn't right, but every time I talked to him I would just melt. At times I found myself making pleas to God that somehow He would make it work. Other times, I tried to talk myself out of my feelings for him by reminding myself of all the things that weren't right. But none of it changed the feeling I would get when he was around.

I told you this was going to get real.

During that time I was reading about Jesus's crucifixion. In Matthew 26 Jesus is praying in the Garden of Gethsemane. In verse 39 it says,

> *"Then he walked a short distance away, and overcome with grief, he threw himself facedown on the ground and prayed, 'My Father, if there is any way you can deliver me from this suffering, please take it from me. Yet what I want is not important, for I only desire to fulfill your plan for me.' Then an angel from heaven appeared to strengthen Him" (TPT).*

Even though Jesus already knew the plan of action from heaven, He still poured out His heart's desire to His Father. He let God know that dying was really not what He wanted to do that day. Yet, it didn't stop there. He told God, "Not my will but Your will be done." Even though He knew it would be contrary to what He wanted, He still chose God's desire over His own. Then, I believe the angel gave Him the strength He needed to do the Father's will.

It's a good thing the angel strengthened Him because He needed a lot of self-control for what would happen next. His betrayer came and God's plan moved forward for Jesus' crucifixion. Then, when one of His disciples took a swing at one of the soldiers and sliced off his ear, what was Jesus' reaction? He didn't say, "thanks dude, I really don't want to do this." He said,

> *"Put your dagger away...Don't you realize that I could ask my heavenly Father for angels to come at any time to deliver me? And instantly He would answer me by sending twelve armies of the angelic host to come and protect us. But that would thwart the prophetic plan of God. For it has been written that it would happen this way"* (Matthew 26:52b-54, ESV).

Jesus had the power to put an end to all of it at any given moment! But He chose to follow through with God's plan even though it was contrary to His own.

After reading that, I decided to try out Jesus's thing. I poured out my heart to the Father about what I was feeling for the guy and what my heart really wanted. I even made a list of what I wanted in a husband. I made sure to be specific too, not watering it down to what was practical to ask for. I invited Him into my desires and expectations for what my future marriage would look like. But then I gave it over to Him. I told Him that more than all those things, I wanted His will to be done, and I asked Him to give me the desire and the strength to do it.

Did my feelings for that guy go away after that? Nope. But I really felt the grace of God continually reminding me that His plan is so much better. And His presence gave me the strength time and time again to choose that plan.

Obeying God doesn't mean we become robots, ready to mindlessly do whatever He requests without shedding a tear. God doesn't expect us to not have expectations, or hopes or desires. Those things make us who we are! But He does ask us to give Him lordship over those things. He asks us to surrender those things to Him so that they don't take the throne that He is supposed to occupy in our hearts. And because when we give them to Him, it gives Him permission to be intimately involved in our lives.

CHAPTER SIX

Trust and Obey

The beautiful thing is that God doesn't always deny us the things we want. We see this in the life of Abraham. Like we saw before, he waited a long time for his promise and went through a lot before Isaac was finally born. The story could have ended there with a nice, happy ending. But God wasn't just in it for the promise to be fulfilled. He wanted to make sure He had Abraham's heart. Suddenly, when Isaac was a teenager, God spoke to Abe. He told him to take his son, go for one last father-son hike, and then make him a human sacrifice. This is the first time Isaac is mentioned since his birth. There was no built up expectation that this would be coming, or that this was a part of God's plan. When God gave Abe this command He didn't even explain why. What good could possibly come from it? Why did God need the sacrifice? Didn't Abraham need Isaac more, so that he could fulfill the promise that *God* had actually given him? This one, short command seemed to go completely contrary to everything else God had said to Abe before.

The thing that amazes me is Abraham's response- he didn't have one! Right after God gave him his instructions it says "*Early* the next morning Abraham got up and loaded his donkey" (Genesis 22:3, ESV, emphasis mine). He didn't grumble. He didn't ask questions. He didn't pray about it for another couple weeks. He responded and he responded quickly!

When Abraham brought Isaac to the altar, God sent an angel to stop him from killing the promise. The point is that Abraham was willing to obey God over trying to make his dreams come true. He trusted God's heart and that He would make the promise happen even if the odds were against it and nothing made sense. He trusted God's way. I guess Abraham learned his lesson from sleeping with Hagar, birthing Ishmael, and trying to make things work on his own.

In the years of waiting, in the years of failure, in the years of wandering, in the years of progress, and in the years of seeing the promise, Abraham learned to trust God. He saw that God was for him.

Often, our problem with obedience is that we don't really trust God. We are believers who don't believe. If we really trusted God fully, we wouldn't struggle to obey Him. Worship leader Melissa Helser says, "If you trust God's character, you won't question His motives."

Hundreds of years later, Abraham's promised offspring struggled to have his same faith in God. As they left their promised land and wandered in the wilderness, we see their struggle to fully obey God. They continually questioned, complained to, and rebelled against God and their leaders.

In Numbers 13 and 14, we read the report of the spies who went to check out the promised land. This passage is very familiar because the words of these twelve guys are what determined the next forty years for Israel. When Moses sent them out he gave them a command, "Be of good courage..." (Numbers 13:20, ESV). But when the spies returned they shared what they saw. At first, it seemed to be a good report detailing how great the fruit of the land was, but then they began to focus on their limitations. Despite Caleb and Joshua trying to lighten the mood and encourage the people, the complaints of the other ten spies just got more and more negative. There's a difference between stating limitations from a perspective of knowing they can be overcome and complaining about limitations from a position of defeat. The majority of the spies were doing the latter.

After all the good things God had done to bring them out of Egypt, and after Moses' command to "be of good courage" they still didn't believe they would get their promised land. They actually believed that God would lead them all the way to the edge of their promised land just so they could be killed trying to take it!

As I was reading this story a while ago I got tears in my eyes and felt the ache of God's heart for His people, and I heard the Father say, "They didn't believe that I was good."

After all He did for them.

Like a prince rescuing his princess from a tall tower, God had pursued the Israelites in their captivity and broke them free with extravagantly performed marvelous deeds. Maybe they forgot who it was they were following. Maybe they believed He had been good but that His goodness wouldn't be enough to stretch out to the wilderness and bring them into the Promised Land. Maybe they knew that God *could* win the battle for them, but they didn't trust that He *would*. Whatever the case, in some place in their hearts there was some belief that the God they followed had a character capable of going out of His way just to lead them to their death before they tasted of the land of milk and honey.

During the three years I spent in Thailand, God began to train me and put me in a position of leading worship. I had always had a heart to worship Him but never dreamed of or planned on becoming a worship leader. One day I was reflecting on my role as a worship leader and I asked God why He led me to focus so strongly on that ministry for those three years. He answered by showing me that every time I lead worship, I became stronger in my foundational belief in knowing that He is good.

Every week I had to get up in front of a group of people and encourage them to worship God. I had to have a fresh revelation of who He was to me so that I could impart that fresh revelation to the people I was leading. There were weeks where I would get a text message from a family member with sad or distressing news just minutes before I would get up to lead worship. There were Saturday nights that I would be weeping because I didn't feel like God was answering my prayers for my family, my ministry, or my own life, but still I led people to sing choruses declaring His goodness the next morning.

I used to be very confused by David. I didn't understand how in the same song he could praise God exuberantly and then complain about his enemies and heartaches. I didn't understand how in one breath he could both express his love to God and also say "God why are you far from me?" Then one day I got it.

I was so overwhelmed during that time. I felt as though there were so many attacks against the ministry I was doing and at the same time there were things happening in my family. I was so discouraged and frustrated, I just began to cry during a time of worship. Suddenly I got a picture of myself standing hunched over, weeping, with hands raised to God. The enemy's arrows were coming at me from all sides, but I knew that he couldn't harm me. I knew there was something deep inside my core, a piece of hope, that was still testifying of the goodness of God.

I became aware then that the enemy couldn't take my faith in who God is. He could take everything that I had. He could attack my body, my mind, and my heart, but as long as I knew God, *Really* knew Him, then I wouldn't be destroyed. I would be like David, genuinely praising God in the midst of surrounding enemies and completely overwhelming seasons.

We can easily look at the Israelites and their wavering faith that cost them forty years of wandering and judge them. How could they not believe in God after He did so much for them? How could they question the One who led them with a cloud by day and pillar of fire by night? But often I've seen that I'm exactly the same way. As soon as I see the enemy or the obstacles, I question God's heart for me. Often when I need to fight a little bit or wait or step out, I become more focused on my fear than on who my God is.

But I want to be like Caleb, of whom God said,

"But My servant Caleb, because he has a different spirit and has followed Me fully, I will bring into the land into which he entered, and his descendants shall take possession of it" (Numbers 14:24, ESV).

I want to stand before a land of giants and say "lets go get it!" I want to walk in a different spirit, unshaken by questions and doubts and fears. I want to see God's kindness, goodness, greatness more than I see the problems, lack, and loss.

To have that different spirit, a spirit that is willing and ready to obey, I need to get with God. I need to understand and believe His heart for me is good. Even when no one else does.

CHAPTER SEVEN

My Desert, My Gift

We don't often consider our dry seasons to be a time to celebrate. Often we don't approach them with excitement or anticipation. Actually, when we start to feel the heat of the desert, we turn around and try to run as fast as we can in the opposite direction. I know I would much rather have my feet propped up next to a swimming pool with a book and a frappe in hand. Anyone else with me?

As I'm sure I illustrated sufficiently, I wasn't exactly gung-ho on moving to Thailand. Thailand had messed with my plans and got in the way of me and my "real destiny." I went there with a feeling that I was walking into my wilderness season. But as I shared a few chapters ago, I made a commitment, a decision, to "marry the land." If God was going to put me in that place, I was going to show Him that I wasn't just going to obey Him begrudgingly, but I was going to be all in. I didn't want to go in counting down the days until my two year training would be complete and I could move on with my life. I was going to suck the life out of every moment, every experience, and I was going to make some friends while I did it.

The Israelites got stuck in the wilderness for forty years because they had a bad attitude in the wilderness. An entire generation died out there and never even got to see the promise, the point of all their struggles. I did *not* want that to happen to me. So instead, I dove right in.

The thing is, I had no idea how much I would come to love Thailand. When I had almost completed my two-year commitment there, I received a very sincere and generous compliment from a visiting missionary regarding my ability to speak Thai and adapt in such a short amount of time. I had done part of my training with this missionary before leaving for Thailand and we hadn't seen each other in over two years. He is from Russia and is very experienced with translating languages. Many people had complimented me on my ability to pick up the language, but his compliment sank deeply into my heart.

Later, I pondered his words and the effect they had on me and I suddenly realized, after two years, how much I had come to love the Thai people with the love of the Father. Learning the language had connected me to their heart. Tears started to flow as I thought about how I had given a piece of my heart to Thailand and how one day I would have to leave. The very place I resisted going, had become the place I would resist leaving.

This isn't to say that that season was a piece of cake. It surely wasn't. It was a training ground where I was challenged in so many ways. I'll share some of the stories in the chapters to come. But in the midst of the trials, the breaking, and the waiting, there was SO. MUCH. GRACE. There was grace to learn the language, grace to build relationships, grace to walk in leadership, grace to start things, grace to grow, grace to be full of joy even in the midst of trials and patience even in the midst of waiting. In between some of the hardest moments, came some of the most beautiful ones.

However, over the years I've seen people come and go who haven't thrived. Even people who felt a strong calling and desire to be in Thailand who never made it or who came and went home before they planned. People who have had extreme culture shock and have struggled with the language. People who have battled sickness and spiritual attack around every corner. People who have had to fight every day for their calling and destiny in this nation. It's not a judgment on them, many endured things that I can't even imagine facing!

But it caused me to question: why me?

Why did the language come easy to me when I didn't have long-term plans to use it? Why did I feel so at home when I didn't even want to be in that nation in the first place? Why did I so easily come to love the people whom I didn't even think God was "calling me" to minister to?

And God answered.

He said, "You obediently followed me into the desert, so I made your desert season into your gift."

After Isaac's close call with his dad's knife, he grew up and started a family of his own. He was starting to see the fulfillment of the promises God made to Abraham. But first, he had to have his own faith tested. This came through a time of famine in the land, as we see in Genesis 26. Isaac went to go find food and the Lord spoke to him, instructing him not to go to Egypt, but to settle down right in the area that his father had once lived and that would later become his descendant's promised land. He stayed there and I must say, he cleaned house! In a time where there was famine all around, he sowed and in the same year reaped a hundredfold! He made a lot of money off of his crops, but he made some enemies too.

In order to get between Isaac and his blessings, the Philistines did their best to cut off his water supply. Sometimes these days with our faucets and abundance of running water we forget that *water is life*. They pushed him into a dry season, which could potentially destroy him and all his possessions.

First, they kicked him out of their land. I'm not sure how they did it, maybe they refused to give him access to their water wells. Whatever they did, Isaac obeyed their wishes and left. He went to a place where his own father had once sojourned, the Valley of Gerar. Abe had dug a lot of wells in that region, so maybe Isaac thought it would be easy to relocate there. He didn't know that his enemies had gone back and filled in all of Abraham's wells after he died. Isaac went back and had to re-dig them all.

Digging wells was not a cheap or easy job. It was costly and time-consuming, but necessary. Isaac went through the dirty work to get the wells back in order that his father and his family had once used. He even kept the names that his father had given them. He had restored his family legacy.

But there was more. He found something even more precious, wells of flowing water. These were a hot commodity on the market in those days, and his servants had found some!

However, the first well they discovered was called "quarreling" because the Philistine herdsman claimed it as their own and wouldn't back down. The servants moved on and found another well, this one was called "enmity" because, again it was taken over by their enemies. Finally, though, they discovered a well that no one else fought over. It belonged to Isaac and it was called "broad places".

The flowing water that Isaac had been searching and fighting for was finally discovered in a broad place, a place far enough away from civilization that no one else wanted it. I believe this broad place was like a wilderness. It was uninhabited, far removed, and unwanted. And Isaac had to go to this place to get to a well, a deep connection to living water, that couldn't be stolen from him. The blessing was found where no one else wanted to go.

There are treasures that God has hidden for us in our wilderness seasons that are far better than the things we've found in the past. There are greater depths of Him that He has for us to dig into. There is growth and expansion and inheritance. But it all depends on the posture of our hearts.

I'm not trying to paint a picture of an easy wilderness. It's not all fun and games. When I moved to Thailand, I felt like God was leading me in a direction completely opposite of His promises and my dreams. There were times I felt lonely, misunderstood, and frustrated. I was constantly being asked to step out of my comfort zone, and things were continually being exposed and corrected in my heart. However, God was doing so much during that time that I couldn't deny that He was blessing me right there in the midst of my desert wandering.

There are certainly seasons where you can't see those blessings or His presence so clearly. My point is that no matter how hard or dry your season is, it's the posture of your heart that will bring the fruit in due time. And when you are walking in obedience to Him, your desert doesn't have to be miserable.

"For I've kept my eyes focused on his righteous words and I've obeyed everything that he's told me to do. I've done my best to be blameless and to follow all his ways, keeping my heart pure. I've kept my integrity by surrendering to him. And so the Lord has rewarded me with his blessing. This is the treasure I discovered when I kept my heart clean before his eyes" (Psalm 18:22-24, TPT).

The Lord hasn't brought you to the wilderness just to survive, He's brought you there to test and produce something in you. If you walk into the wilderness with the mindset of just passing time, waiting for your "big break" into your promised land, you will either get stuck in that desert for a long time or God will keep bringing you back there until you leave transformed.

My competitive nature doesn't like the thought of not passing a test or not getting the most out of an opportunity which in a way was a good thing. It caused me to be determined and persistent for all that God had for me in Thailand. I didn't want to settle and I didn't want to just get by.

A mentor shared a picture that she had of me when I first moved to Thailand and it has stuck with me over the years. She saw me walking on a path towards a destination. On both sides of the path it was dirty and muddy, but every few steps I would stop and veer off the path a bit to dig something up. As I dug it out and cleaned all the dirt off, you could see that it was a bright, shining gem. I would take the gem and stick it to myself and continue on down the path until I stopped to find another gem. She said that those gems represented the character and heart of God. I had to slow down, even pause my pursuit of the destination to dig them up, but then they became a part of my character as well. I began to shine like He shines.

God has some great things in store for you in the midst of whatever season you are walking through: revelations, anointing, memories, character traits, fruit of the Spirit, and so much more. Let's become archeologists of His character during our tough seasons. Let's become those who are longing to discover His heart more than we long for our destination. Let's determine that we don't want to leave the wilderness empty handed or defeated, but leave shining more than when we came.

CHAPTER EIGHT

Wilderness Invitation

Now I'm in a completely different sort of wilderness. It caught me completely off guard since, in the natural, I'm stepping into my "promised land." I moved to Nepal this year. Finally. Six years have passed since the first time I came to Nepal and knew that it would become my home, and it's been three and a half years since I first set out to move to Thailand. This is the long-awaited season where I will begin to step into my destiny.

Early on in my growing relationship with the Lord, whenever we sang songs at church about surrender I would get this picture of myself in a white space. It wasn't a room. It seemed to go on and on into the distance, but it was completely empty. Only I was there, with nothing and no one else. Standing in the midst of nothingness for all eternity. This picture was like an invitation from God, but it was also like a test. It was as if God was asking me, "If this was you and you had only my presence, would it really be enough for you?"

Is He really enough for me? I never really knew the answer.

Leading up to this big transition in my life I was struggling with some anxiety and fears. I was very aware that I was coming to Nepal alone. That I was leaving a big team, a lot of friends, an established ministry, and my second home. That I was stepping out of the boat. And there were some things that I thought God was going to work out on my behalf beforehand that, well...He didn't. So one day, as I was driving in America on a visit before the move, I just began to pour out all my expectations and needs before Him. I told Him, "God if you don't fill these needs externally, I need you to show me that you are enough. I need to hear you like I've never heard you before, see you more clearly than I've ever seen you before, feel you so close that I can't deny you are with me."

Now I'm here. This season that I've been waiting for for so long, yet it doesn't feel like what I expected. I'm in the midst of cultural immersion, staying with an amazing Nepali family. However, despite my proficiency in the Thai language and my progress in building relationships and rapport there, I am back at square one here. I have no ministry and no job description. I went from a full day of meetings and outreaches in Thailand, often returning home after a 12 hour day, to taking at least one nap a day and reading a book a week. I went from being a part of two thriving teams, to being a "team" of one. Friendships that had developed over three years are now reduced to text messages, just like my friendships in America. And I have had to start over with introductions, small talk, and the process of slowly opening up to people. My apartment that I had come to love and all my belongings got narrowed down to a couple of suitcases which I couldn't unpack fully in my small room. I walked into this place having been stripped of positions, recognition, relationships, ministries, independence, belongings, and yet still carrying so much. Still holding so many "things" to comfort my heart, just in case He's not enough for me.

I've started to see that I can't see God pull through for me when I'm holding to other things. I'll never know if He's enough if I never need Him to be my everything. He might have enough provision when I have financial lack, or enough wisdom when I need guidance, but I won't know if He is fully enough unless I need Him to be.

"But he also can turn a barren wilderness into an oasis with water! He can make springs flow into desert lands and turn them into fertile valleys so that cities spring up, and he gives it all to those who are hungry" (Psalm 107:35-36 TPT).

It's often not until we get to a place of desperation and desolation that we truly learn to hunger for Him. And then, after we've sincerely hungered and sought after Him, He meets us in our need and we'll see wells of His presence spring up in the wastelands.

In the book of Hosea, God takes extreme measures to show us how He pursues His Bride, Israel. Even when she strayed from Him and tried to fill her desires with other lovers, He wooed her back. His tactics for wooing her didn't seem all that nice though. He didn't just give her more nice gifts or talk sweet to her. First, He stripped her of everything. He surrounded her with desolation and pain, took away all the blessings and glamor of her past life, and made her experience rejection and embarrassment. Then He led her out into the wilderness.

The thing is, He did it all in His grace and mercy. It would have been cruel for Him to leave her to her wistful desires, with her lovers that would satisfy for only a moment. But it was His grace that caused her to experience the pain and brokenness of the wilderness, so that He could take her back into His arms.

"And now, here's what I'm going to do:

I'm going to start all over again.

I'm taking her back out into the wilderness

where we had our first date, and I'll court her.

I'll give her bouquets of roses.

I'll turn Heartbreak Valley into Acres of Hope.

She'll respond like she did as a young girl,

those days when she was fresh out of Egypt."

(Hosea 2:14-15 MSG)

God doesn't drag us into the wilderness. He invites us.

The enemy doesn't force us into the wilderness either. We often blame the devil for our hard seasons, we complain about our trials, and we avoid being alone. But what brought Jesus into the desert?

"Then Jesus was led up by the Spirit into the wilderness to be tempted by the devil" (Matthew 4:1, ESV).

That's Spirit with a capital "S." It was the Spirit of God that led Jesus into the wilderness to be tempted and tested.

God is inviting us to come and meet Him in the secluded places that no one else wants to go, the hidden places, the wide open spaces, because He wants to woo us there. He wants to bring us into a greater depth of intimacy. He wants to test us to see if He is really our everything. He wants to show us that He really is all we need.

We don't usually see the idols that we have built in our own hearts. Maybe they didn't start off as idols but gradually began to grip us with a stronger and stronger hold, until we felt we couldn't live without them. The thing is, we don't usually know they have such a grip on us until we try to pry ourselves away from them, or until they are stripped away from us. I know that when I'm not joyfully willing to lay something down for God, it has become an idol in my heart.

Even the words or promises God has given us can become idols if we value them more than we value God or what He's speaking to us now. One of my friends, Grace Hufton, recently stated in her podcast "Single and Lovin' It" that we have to put "the Promiser over the Promise, *always*." Time and time again, God has asked me to lay down my dream of moving to Nepal in order to experience His best for me. At the time it was difficult, the dream was put on the altar and soaked with a lot of tears. Now the dream has been resurrected, and it is beautiful, but it isn't my everything and I'm so grateful to God for that.

He and I are not stopping there. Like I said before, I walked into this season still carrying things, idols that had snuck in a long time ago that I had never even noticed. When I was a child I had a blanket I carried with me everywhere. I would rub the silk edges on my lip until the edge frayed and began falling apart. It was my comfort for scary, uncomfortable, or even just boring moments. In the same way I was attached to that blanket, I clung to some desires, identities, and control as I began to navigate all this new territory.

But God has loosened my grip on even those few things I carried with me into this season. Some things were stripped away, some things He asked me to lay down. Some days I've been better at laying them down than others. However, more than feeling like He is cruel or trying to hurt me, I feel His love stronger than ever. It's His grace that does what's necessary to bring me into a deeper relationship with Him. It's His goodness that won't allow me to stay where I am. It's His love that pursues me in the wilderness.

On my birthday, the week before I moved, I asked God for a word for this year. He told me, "Nepal is my gift for you, to bless you. It's not just your assignment. That nation will do more in and for you this year than you will do for it. Receive my gift."

He is the gift in the desert. I get to know His ways more. I get to spend time seeking His face. I get to have barriers in my heart torn down and idols uprooted so that nothing will hinder intimacy with Him.

Now let's look at Moses and the Israelites again. After they escaped from Egypt and spent a bit of time in the desert, they camped out at Mount Sinai for a bit while God gave Moses some detailed instructions. As many of us know, they got anxious waiting for Moses and they had Aaron build a golden calf for them to worship. After God had JUST told them not to make any images or worship any other gods.

As you can imagine God was a bit angry with them. However, this sin is not what kept the Israelites from the Promised Land! God's punishment for them was different. He said, "Go up to a land flowing with milk and honey; but I will not go up among you, lest I consume you on the way, for you are a stiff-necked people" (Exodus 33:3, ESV).

Ouch. He essentially said, "Here, take your blessed land, but I'm not going to hang out where I'm unwanted!"

It's a good thing that Moses was a man who knew how to seek after God's heart. We see his desperation in his response to God in verses 15-16,

> "And he said to him, 'If your presence will not go with me, do not bring us up from here. For how shall it be known that I have found favor in your sight, I and your people? Is it not in your going with us, so that we are distinct, I and your people, from every other people on the face of the earth?'"

He decided that it would be better to be in a forsaken land with the presence of God in their midst than to be in a land flowing with milk and honey and be forsaken by Him.

God saw Moses's desire for Him and it moved Him. He responded by saying, "This very thing that you have spoken I will do, for you have found favor in my sight, and I know you by name."

David had the same heart. He wrote a psalm when he was in a tight place, with his enemy constantly trying to take his life. He cries out to God about his problems, asking God to protect him from His enemies. But in the end listen to what he says, "Your godly lovers will thank you no matter what happens. For they choose and cherish your presence above everything else" (Psalm 140:13, TPT).

So, here's the thing: If this whole wilderness thing still isn't looking great to you, you might need to ask yourself what cost you are willing to pay to meet Him. Will you obey Him even if it means letting go of other seemingly good things? Will you thank Him for His presence even when that's all you have? If you see Him standing in the midst of the desert, will you run to meet Him or run away the second you feel the heat?

CHAPTER NINE

Worth the Battles

Our obedience doesn't just lead us into the wilderness, sometimes it leads us into the battlefield. I believe there is grace when we obey God, however, He doesn't promise us it will be a piece of cake either. The thing He does promise us is that He's with us in the battles, just like He is with us in the wilderness.

I was in a season that seemed like it was packed full of battle after battle. In our village outreach in Thailand the one man who had actually received Jesus and was being discipled went to prison, leaving his teenage son with no one to take care of him. We stepped in, and I learned that what my parents always said is true, parenting teenagers is no joke! Not to mention a teenager with a very broken family background and a father in prison! He started to act out and get into trouble before eventually running away.

Meanwhile, the other progress we thought we were making in the outreach seemed to be coming to a halt or moving quickly in the opposite direction. The worship team I was leading was having its challenges. I had prepared everything well to begin to transition to Nepal, nevertheless I was left with no one to pass the responsibilities to. I was facing some hard things in my family as well, which tends to shake me emotionally even on the other side of the world.

One morning in my office I reached the end of myself. I couldn't pull myself together and stop crying. All I wanted to do was run out of the mess, away from all my responsibilities, and hide. I was tired and frustrated and, honestly, feeling sorry for myself. I felt like I didn't have anything left to give so I might as well just stop trying.

But in that moment God spoke, like He always does. This time He didn't give me a verbal pat on the back or urge me to pick myself up, instead He very graciously corrected me by reminding me of something He spoke to me a couple weeks before.

In Jeremiah 15, starting in verse 15, Jeremiah is pouring his heart out to God unreservedly, much like David always did. I'll be referencing this passage in the Amplified Version of the Bible, which just expands our understanding of the text by trying to encompass more of the meaning from the original Hebrew using parentheses and brackets. Basically, in this passage Jeremiah is saying to God, "Look at me! Don't forget how willing I was to serve you and how much I gave up, but now it seems like you're punishing me! I'm taking a lot of clout for you!" And I don't blame Jeremiah. The things he was saying were true. If you read the rest of his book you'll see that Jeremiah had to bring some pretty heavy and depressing messages to the people, and he was pretty alone in it. That's why he was called the weeping prophet. Poor Jeremiah. He ends his rant with this verse: "Why has my pain been perpetual and my wound incurable, refusing to be healed? Will you indeed be to me like a deceptive brook with water that is unreliable?" (Jeremiah 15:18, AMP).

I can imagine Jeremiah was saying what I was thinking in that overwhelming moment: "I didn't sign up for all this, it's nothing like you told me it was going to be." Many of us reach this point when we step out in obedience to God. We make the initial sacrifices and walk it out for a while but usually before the fruit comes we face the opposition. We still aren't seeing what was promised to us, instead we're facing fiery darts from the enemy on every side. We think that God is being unfair for making us face these kinds of battles when we are serving Him. Isn't He the one who called us here anyways?

Most people are familiar with how God called Jeremiah, because He spoke some pretty big things over him. We like to quote those verses and declare them over our own lives. But did God promise Jeremiah that people wouldn't be mad at him? Or that his mission would be easy to carry out? Nope! He said, "Do not be afraid of them [or their hostile faces], for I am with you [always] to protect you and deliver you" (Jeremiah 1:8, AMP).

God was essentially saying, "Even though you'll have people who hate you and even though life will be rough for you *I* will be there with you in all of it. Even if it looks like more people are against you than for you, just know that I am for you and that's enough."

So let's fast-forward, back to Jeremiah's rant in chapter 15. How do you think God responded to Jeremiah? Maybe not how you expect. His words put Jeremiah in his place and they are also what brought correction to my own heart in the midst of my pity party.

> *"Therefore, thus says the Lord [to Jeremiah], 'If you repent [and give up this mistaken attitude of despair and self-pity], then I will restore you [to a state of inner peace] so that you may stand before Me [as My obedient representative]; and if you separate the precious from the worthless [examining*

yourself and cleansing your heart from unwarranted doubt concerning My faithfulness], you will become My spokesman. Let the people turn to you [and learn to value My values]- but you, you must not turn to them [with regard for their idolatry and wickedness]'" (Jeremiah 15:19, AMP).

Ouch.

There are times when God speaks to us gently and compassionately, and other times He gives us the kick in the butt we need to get out of our pit! And that's exactly what He did for Jeremiah. He still had more that He wanted to do with Jeremiah but He needed him to be able to stand in faith in the middle of all the accusations.

Graham Cooke said, "We need to stop treating life's difficulties as if they shouldn't be happening to us." We are soldiers in a war! When a soldier enlists in the military he isn't surprised when he is sent into battle! It's part of what he signed up for!

Many of us have already said a whole-hearted "yes" to God's call on our lives. All those good promises He spoke of the great things He wants to do with us sounded pretty good. But we need to realize what we signed up for, read between the lines. In the list of things God gave us to do, He didn't promise us that we wouldn't need to fight for them. For most of us, He didn't say that everyone would support our vision. So when we face some hard stuff along the way and we start to feel hopeless and sorry for ourselves, He is waiting for us to repent and come in alignment with Him. Then He will be able to give us peace and lead us into what He called us to do.

The enemy meets us in these pinnacle moments to tell us that God isn't faithful and that He's untrustworthy, or that He must not have really called us. He blinds us with our current circumstances, trying to convince us that they are an indication of where we are headed. Just like the Israelites right after they got out of Egypt and got cornered between the Red Sea and the army of Egyptians. They immediately doubted God and what He promised to do saying,

> *"Is it because there are no graves in Egypt that you have taken us away to die in the wilderness? What is this that you have done to us by bringing us out of Egypt?...For it would have been better for us to serve the Egyptians [as slaves] than to die in the wilderness" (Exodus 14:11-12, AMP).*

Moses responded by encouraging them,

> *"The Lord will fight for you while you [only need to] keep silent and remain calm." Meanwhile God challenged them, "Why do you cry to me? Tell the sons of Israel to move forward..." (Exodus 14:14-15, AMP)*

When we are in these situations, the enemy wants us either to turn back to the place where we came from, or to freeze and allow our fear to consume us. But our Father, and good leaders in our lives, continue to encourage us and keep us moving forward.

God in His grace often asks for our obedience when we are in a place of courage and anticipation for what's to come. But we need to determine to continue to follow in obedience even if everything is coming against us. If we want to be used by God, it's not a matter of waiting for the hardships and frustrations to end, but instead learning to stand in the midst of them.

If God really called us, we need to decide that His call is worth taking a stand for. His call is worth the battles we will have to walk through. We need to remind ourselves, "I signed up for this! And I'm not going to give into the hopelessness and fear that comes from the enemy!" And when we position ourselves in that way God meets us with His perfect peace and His presence. Just like He promised Jeremiah, He promises us His companionship. He is with us to protect us and deliver us.

When your obedience leads you right into the thick of the battle, remember that He is worth it. His promises that He gave you when He called you are still worth it.

One picture that helps me through the battles is from Psalm 23:5, "You prepare a table before me in the presence of my enemies." Can you just imagine that? Imagine being in a war and you waltz into the enemy's camp, past all the soldiers standing outside their tents with their guns in hand, and in the middle of it all you see an elaborate table set out with all of your favorite foods. There your Good Shepherd sits, ready to feast with you.

The battles don't seem as overwhelming when you know that you fight them by...*eating*! Whenever the battle raging around me starts to get overwhelming I picture myself feasting on the goodness, love, and grace of the Father. I lock eyes with Him, even as the enemies of fear, doubt, and weariness are crowding around me. We fight by resting and trusting in Him. Just like Moses told the Israelites, "The Lord will fight for you, you need only to remain silent."

So after you've taken the initial steps of obedience, keep obeying. If you walk through the wilderness, keep choosing to pursue Him and His heart. If you encounter battles, keep your "yes" to Him. He's fighting for you. He is with you. And He makes it all worth it.

CHAPTER TEN

The Fruit of One "Yes"

Fifty years ago everything changed in a very remote village of Nepal because of one man who was impacted by one woman.

The man, from a small village, worked as a porter, carrying the bags of visiting trekkers. His job once brought him to Pokhara, a major city in Nepal. On this trip he met a woman who worked in a Christian missionary hospital. She heard the gospel through a missionary and shared what she knew with him. She also taught him that if he prayed in Jesus' name that Jesus could heal sickness.

Suddenly, while in Pokhara, the man received news that his son was very sick, things weren't looking good for him. The family had done everything that their history and culture told them to do. They took him to witch doctors and Hindu and Buddhist priests and performed every ritual that was asked of them, to no avail. None of their efforts were fruitful and the son continued to deteriorate. So the man returned home to the village and decided to act on what the Christian had told him. He shut himself in a room with his son in the evening and stayed there three nights, praying for his son in the name of Jesus. The next morning his son was completely healed!

This man gave his life to the Lord after the incident and one by one so did the members of his family. However, this shook the status quo for the village. They didn't know anything about Jesus, but they knew it challenged their ancient customs and beliefs. The people of the village began to severely persecute the man and his brother. They were eventually driven out of the village and forced to live in caves for a few years. They would return to the village by night to meet their families, share Jesus with them, and get the supplies they needed to continue to dwell in their hiding places.

During this time, a woman in the village became very sick. Again, they did all they knew to do for her to be healed. They consulted all the religious leaders and spirits, to no avail. So the village leaders made a decision. They called the two Christian men from their cave dwelling and made a deal with them. They asked them to come pray for the woman with the promise: "If she's healed, we'll accept your God. But if not, we're going to kill you."

For most of us, our obedience doesn't lead us to a situation with these kinds of stakes! These men could have run. Maybe they could have weighed their odds and split, but they didn't. They stayed and they prayed.

Of course, God responded to the faith and obedience of these men. They prayed for the woman all night, and sure enough, the next morning she was healed. Now, the majority of that village and a lot of that whole district are now Christian. The amount of faith and boldness these men had, in that situation and throughout their lives afterwards, inspires me. But I want to highlight someone else in that story. The woman working in the hospital in Pokhara.

She was probably just a normal person, maybe even a new believer. Yet, in a time when the nation was hostile to the gospel, she took a risk and shared with her Buddhist Animist friend. She didn't know what kind of fruit it would produce. She wasn't trying to save a whole village. She was just being obedient with the opportunity God placed before her, and if she hadn't we can only guess that the son would have died, as would the older woman, and the village would still be unreached. I'm now staying and doing ministry with the nephew of that first believer. After being persecuted, his uncle left the village and his dad and other uncle continued the work of the gospel, living in caves and eventually pioneering the church in that area. This woman's obedience affected the trajectory of my life here in Nepal over fifty years later.

God gives us many opportunities to obey Him throughout our day. Opportunities to hear His voice and respond in faith. Some of these feel significant when we reach them while others don't seem like a big deal. But obedience is always a big deal. We never know what kind of waves we are creating with one drop of obedience. We never know what kind of fruit will be produced from one seed called "yes".

When we say yes to God in the little things, we are building trust with Him. When we get a slight urge to pick up a piece of trash on the street or to take the longer way to work or to buy a latte for a friend and we don't ignore it but we actually *do it*, it shows God that we are paying attention. It shows Him that we're willing to put in a bit of extra effort to take a risk and do something that might mean nothing. Then, I believe, the urges start to be for more significant things: giving someone at work a hundred dollar bill, sharing the Gospel with a friend, giving a prophetic word to your waitress. When those bigger opportunities for obedience present themselves, your faith muscles are exercised and you can trust it's Him because of all the little moments that you obeyed and it proved to be fruitful.

I like to practice hearing God's voice when I have free time on my day off. I sometimes just want to go to a coffee shop and read, or watch Netflix all afternoon, but more than how I feel, I want to spend time with God. So I'll ask Him, "God what should we do today? Where do you want to go?" Sometimes I don't really sense anything except that He's giving me permission to rest. Other times I'll have an urge to go somewhere I wouldn't normally go. Once in Thailand I felt an urge to go to this art museum that I had never been to before. I love going on adventures, but I don't usually like to try out a new place on my own. Even though it was out of my comfort zone, I went. The whole time I was paying attention, communing with the Holy Spirit in case He had someone He wanted me to meet or minister to while I was there. I got nothing.

I almost let disappointment settle in, wondering if I had heard God correctly to go to that specific museum. Or if I missed someone I should have spoken to while there. But I knew through that experience He was exercising my faith muscles and reminding me that He wants to do life with me like that every day. I believe the time I spent driving 30 minutes each way on my scooter in the hot Thailand sun, the time I just lingered in that museum waiting to see if He would speak, and my willingness to do it, were all worship. It was an afternoon spent in worship without a guitar and outside of the church.

The thing I love about God is that He uses our small "yeses" to strengthen our faith and teach us obedience, but He also moves in ways that we don't even know through those moments. Sometimes we see the fruit of our obedience, and other times we can trust that perhaps there was something God did that we had absolutely no idea about. I think maybe the hospital worker in Pokhara didn't have any idea what happened as a result of her obedience. Maybe she felt a lot like I did after I stepped out to go to the museum. That's why it is so crucial that we say yes to whatever whispers God speaks into our hearts.

We say *yes* more often than we may realize, even if we don't verbalize it. We say yes to showing up, to living in the moment, to listening to someone's heart, to giving our all to something, to following the Holy Spirit, and to the little opportunities where nothing is even being asked of us but we choose to give anyways. A yes is as simple as showing up.

The thing is, Jesus is asking for our *yes* not for our success. When He asks something of us He isn't expecting us to produce results; He's asking for us to trust Him in taking the next step. I can so easily overwhelm myself when I try to figure out how to produce fruit, or when I try to get myself to the fulfillment of the dream God has given me. Even the small decisions can stress me out because I wonder how the next step I take will play into the bigger picture, until I remind myself that I'm only responsible to obey in the next step. I don't need to strive to get results and I don't need to see the path all the way to my destination, I only need to keep my heart in a *yes* posture.

All God wants, and all we can give, is our softened, willing hearts. Learning obedience and surrender doesn't usually start with a sudden move to Africa or giving away ten thousand dollars. It starts with answering His call to meet Him. It starts with being there for someone else when you would rather ignore their messages and watch another episode of Gilmore Girls. It starts with giving your friend a twenty when they're raising money for a mission trip. It starts with showing up and choosing to listen to His still small voice throughout your day.

And let me tell you, He sees it. He celebrates over every single *yes* that you say to Him. Even when it seems insignificant to you, He is throwing a party in heaven because His child's heart is turned toward Him. You might not ever see the fruit of your simple obedience on this earth, but you'll get to read all about it in His record book He has awaiting you in heaven!

CHAPTER ELEVEN

Crooked Paths and Hidden Portals

I've said multiple times in my life, "It just feels like God is leading me in the complete opposite direction of His promise for me!" I said it when He changed my plans and led me to go do my internship in Thailand. I said it when He led me to join Go To Nations and return to Thailand. I said it when He led me to lay down more roots in that nation than I thought was necessary.

I've found that first of all, God's purpose isn't to get us to a destination. Even though He's the one who gave us the dream, it's not His number one desire to fulfill that in our lives. If we work in cooperation with Him He *will* fulfill it, because He's God and He doesn't lie, but that's not the aim. His purpose is not to give us promises and then make them happen, as if He were a genie in a bottle, but to live in communion with us, transforming us into His image.

So, while He will bring us from point A to point B, that's not why we're alive. He is so much more concerned with the journey we take with Him to get there. The moments that we get to spend along the way and the seasons that cause us to run to His arms. I think of the allegory *Hinds Feet On High Places* by Hannah Hurnard; the main character, named Much Afraid, goes on a journey through many different environments to get to the high mountain places with the caring Shepherd, who represents Jesus. However, it was in those different seasons that her character was developed and she was prepared. Many times she felt like the Shepherd was far from her, but really he was just a call away. And as she journeyed she began to look more and more like Him. She longed to just arrive and be with Him, but He longed for her to arrive in her true form, the way He created her to be. That's why the journey was necessary.

Secondly, God's path from point A to point B isn't linear. Because He's in no rush to get us to a particular destination, He may take us on a path that makes absolutely no sense to us. We think that the steps we need to take to get to our dream destination are obvious, until we find God is guiding us to do what seems completely contradictory. It's as if we are trying to get from Dallas to LA and God tells us to buy a boat.

When this happens we can start to question if we really heard God to begin with. Am I headed toward the right destination? Is that what He really wanted me to do? Because now it looks like He's leading me somewhere else. Or we try to take control of our journey to the destination by heading in that direction on our own. If He is calling me over here, there's no way He could possibly want me to do that right now. It makes no sense. No this is probably what He really meant.

Let's look again at Proverbs 16. Verses 1-4a say,

> *"Go ahead and make all the plans you want, but it's the Lord who will ultimately direct your steps. We are all in love with our own opinions, convinced they're correct. But the Lord is in the midst of us, testing and probing our every motive. Before you do anything, put your trust totally in God and not in yourself. Then every plan you make will succeed. The Lord works everything together to accomplish his purpose."*

It sounds cliché but God is God, and we are not. How could we limit God to our human reasoning? For us 1+1 always makes 2, but for Him it can make whatever He wants it to make! He can take salt and water and bake a cake! He can lead us North and we can end up in Mexico!

I get this kind of funny picture in my head when I think about this. I honestly don't play video games so I know almost nothing about them, but I'm pretty sure that a lot of games have portals. If you move your character to go stand in a certain spot then press a button, suddenly you will be transported to a completely different location. I think God hides lots of little portals along our journey, but we have to be willing to walk with Him in a random direction, into a corner, or into a hidden place to have access to it. After following Him out of the way, we'll suddenly find that we are a lot closer to our destination than where we started. In order to get to that sudden acceleration, we have to trust where He is taking us in the moment.

If you haven't been able to tell by now, I have mad respect for Moses. What absolutely blows my mind is that he stayed behind the pillar of fire and the pillar of cloud for forty years. *Forty years*! He told God that he didn't want to enter the promised land without His presence, and then he followed that up with forty years of chasing God's presence more than the maps. He would wake up each morning and if the cloud was moving, so would the Israelites. If it stayed, so would they. There probably seemed to be absolutely no rule for how long they stayed or where they went next (as we know they took quite a detour).

At any moment Moses could have said, "Hey look, God said we could go into the promised land years ago, but instead we decided to chase around this cloud. We know where He wants us to be, let's just try and go over there." But he didn't. Even though it meant he would never get to enter the land himself, he never rushed the process or tried to move ahead of God. God zigzagged them all over the place and the Israelites accused Moses of wanting to kill them, but He stayed behind the cloud. We also should look for the cloud, seeking to follow the presence of God wherever He leads.

Even when the land was right before them, after the spies came back with the bad report (like we talked about in Chapter 6), the Israelites tried to show God that they were sorry for not trusting Him and they still wanted to enter the land by going up on their own, but Moses warned them against it. The story is in Numbers 14:

> *"And they rose early in the morning and went up to the heights of the hill country, saying, 'Here we are. We will go up to the place that the Lord has promised, for we have sinned.' But Moses said,*

> *'Why now are you transgressing the command of the Lord, when that will not succeed? Do not go up, for the Lord is not among you, lest you be struck down before your enemies'"* (Numbers 14:40-42 ESV)

Of course, the rebellious Israelites didn't listen and they tried to enter the land, but it didn't end well. They all died.

We read that Moses stayed in the camp with the Ark of the Covenant. He wasn't after the destination, he was after God. And that's how we should be.

Upon moving to Thailand I had a dream. In the dream there was a Nepali boy and a missionary talking. I asked the boy, in English, "How old are you?" And he answered, "Sib pi", which means ten years in Thai. I nodded my head and acknowledged that I understood the boy, and the missionary looked at me, astonished. "How did you understand him?" he asked. I then explained that what he said is the same in the Thai language. The missionary and the boy continued to talk to each other in Nepali and I followed their conversation as some of the words were the same as Thai words.

In reality, the two languages are very very different. So when I woke up from the dream, I asked God, "What does this mean?" And He answered, "Shawna, nothing is wasted. The things you will learn and do in this season will be carried into the next one."

And now I'm seeing the fruit of that promise. I followed God to Thailand when I wanted to be in Nepal, feeling as if I was going in the wrong direction. But God responded to my obedience and used my time in Thailand to impart many valuable things into my heart, as well as to develop many of my gifts that I've carried with me to Nepal. The Israelites' journey to the Promise Land wasn't supposed to take 40 years, but their journey developed their trust in God and taught them to follow Him. Their time in the wilderness wasn't in vain.

I've done so many random things in my short life. I've had a lot of hobbies. Time consuming and expensive ones too. I spent about fourteen years riding and showing horses competitively, played the cello and violin, performed in plays, took Hip Hop dance classes, ran track, wrote stories and songs, took art classes, was involved in 4-H and more. I worked at a BBQ restaurant, nannied and babysat, worked in a warehouse, served as a barista, and led the Children's ministry at my church all before I was twenty-one. I aspired to be a doctor and started taking college courses that would lead me in that direction while I was still in High School.

When I was in Bible school I wondered why I did all that stuff. Why didn't I spend time investing in things that would contribute to my future, to my missionary journey? I did so many things just because it seemed interesting or fun, but what was the purpose in it all? Then, in Thailand, I joined our team performing dances in the Elementary schools we visited. I was involved in dramas to illustrate the Gospel. My history showing horses connected me to unexpected people that would become significant in my life and ministry. I began to lead worship and teach music classes. I often ended up doing children's ministry to some degree wherever I went because that's where the open door was.

Nothing was wasted. Not one thing.

He has a purpose in every seemingly random thing in our lives. The different places He brings us are not an accident or a distraction. They are seasons for us to develop and grow in Him, and they are unexpected steps toward our destination.

If you don't understand where God has you now, trust Him, He knows what He's doing. He hasn't forgotten the things He promised you, but He cares too much about you to take you on the expected path. He wants your heart. He wants to work in mysterious ways. He wants to journey with you on the crooked paths, and He wants to surprise you with hidden portals.

CHAPTER TWELVE

Abundantly More Than You Signed Up For

People used to tell me "If God told you the plans He has for your life all at once you wouldn't be able to handle it." And I liked when people said that, because it communicated to me unfathomable potential. It made my imagination start brimming with signs, wonders, miracles, ministries, reputation, travel, opportunity. It brought to mind the verse that says that the things that Jesus did couldn't be contained in all the world's books and then the verse that says we will do even greater things, and my mind would spin in circles trying to picture that. Like it says in Ephesians 3:20, "exceedingly abundantly above all that we ask or think." I liked the idea that He will do so much more with my life than I could even dream of. I liked the idea that He will take me to the place where a mountain no longer looks big, where the unfathomable has entered the realm of possibility.

However, as I've taken steps toward what God has for me, I'm seeing the statement through a different lens. God certainly has all of those great things in store for me, but He also has had bigger tests, trials, and seasons of process than I could have imagined. While I still have the anticipation of the great promises God has given me for my future, I am realizing that there are big processes on the way to those big promises. I've realized if He showed me right now all that He wanted to do in and through my life and all it would cost me, I probably wouldn't be able to say yes to the sacrifice that would be required on my part. Jesus Himself said in Luke 12:48, "Everyone to whom much was given, of him much will be required, and from him to whom they entrusted much, they will demand the more."

There have been many times that I've surrendered something to God, said yes to Him, and later realized that He was asking more from me than what I originally signed up for. Like when I joined the internship in Thailand, not knowing I would end up joining GTN. The initial "yes" was just the first step of surrender for Him to get me where He wanted me in His perfect will.

One of those times was when God led me to join the worship team in Thailand. I was just starting to sing and play guitar, and had only led worship in small groups with just a few people. I didn't know how to project my voice so when I led worship the sound couldn't be heard beyond a small group of ten, and I definitely didn't know how to work with a band. Then, a few months after moving to Thailand, the worship leader asked me if I would be willing to join the team. I took some time to pray about it, because I didn't consider myself someone who would serve in the worship ministry in a church. It had never crossed my mind. In addition, I knew that I would have to learn to sing the songs in Thai! After some time and pestering from the worship team leader, I decided to join the team in order to be stretched.

I started out singing backup, then eventually leading in English for our prayer meetings, until I finally started learning to lead in Thai for our Sunday services. My journey with worship is a whole other story to tell, but I'll just say that there was a grace and an acceleration for me as I stepped into a calling to lead worship that I didn't even know I had.

After six months on the worship team, my leadership talked to me about assisting the worship leader. She had been really struggling with leading and guiding the team, as well as setting up systems for getting things done. I again took time to pray about it before agreeing to come on for three months as a mentor or advisor for the current worship leader. My main point was that I didn't want to take over leadership, but only support her. Well, within the first month, the worship leader suddenly decided to move back home to the Philippines. It was very unexpected. I can't even remember how everything went down after that. I don't know if there was an official conversation or not, but I ended up filling her role and leading the worship team.

I kind of felt like God tricked me! If He would have asked me to be a worship leader in the beginning I would have said no! But it was actually in His grace that He gave it to me in bite-sized pieces. My fears, reservations, and inabilities would have kept me from a big part of my calling, but my good God didn't want me to miss out on anything He had for me.

God does give us more than we can handle, because our assignment isn't limited to our capacity. He just brings us to that place gradually. He doesn't often plop us into a crazy destiny without the process needed to prepare us.

Some people, when they hear I've been to Nepal, ask me if I've ever climbed Mount Everest. This usually makes me laugh because, while it would be amazing to climb Mount Everest one day, it's no simple feat. The process of actually getting to climb the Mountain can take months of acclimatizing, preparing, and climbing. You have to take multiple trips up and down parts of the mountain face to get your body ready for the final climb. Not to mention spending *at least* a year of physically conditioning and practicing on other peaks before you even see the Mountain. Most people train their whole lives to check Everest off their bucket list. Honestly, I would love to say I've stood on the highest peak in the world, but all of that work doesn't sound very appealing to me.

Now, imagine you could get to the peak of Everest another way. What if a plane or helicopter could fly you up to that point and just drop you off? You could skip over a year of preparations for the instant gratification of the elevated position. But the ecstasy of standing on top of the world wouldn't last long as you begin to have trouble breathing, your lungs begin to fill with fluid, and your brain swells. Your lack of preparation would kill you.

Sorry if that sounds a little extreme. But you wouldn't be able to fly up to Mt. Everest anyway.

So let's think a little more practically. What if you are feeling especially driven and you just decide to hike to the top in one straight hike? Who needs to acclimatize when you are young and strong? I don't think I need to tell you that you would not only struggle with climate sickness, but you would also not have the stamina to make it to the top. Your ambition would essentially kill you.

When you go through the proper procedures to climb Everest, you take into account each leg of the journey and approach it step by step. You keep the peak in your mind and in your vision, but it's not your only goal. You have many other steps and many other goals to get to that point. And at the end of each one you are able to stop, to catch your breath. When you can breathe freely at that stage you are ready for the next one and you can go up higher.

God doesn't put our whole destiny before us to conquer in one shot. He gives us next steps to focus on so we don't need to be overwhelmed with the whole picture, that's for Him to be concerned about. He graciously leads us to the next step needed on the journey and sometimes He gives us a tiny glimpse of where He wants to take us, so we'll know where we are aiming, and other times He just lets us enjoy the surprise!

I've had some of my own experiences with trekking, much more suited for an amateur trekker. I already shared about my first ten day trekking experience and how I had no idea what I was getting into. My last trekking trip was also ten days long, but I was a lot better equipped. I was with a team with a guide and porters, I was in better physical shape, and I had a proper backpack and boots. On the first day we trekked the farthest; about 12 miles, 8 hours of walking. The problem was it had been a long time since I wore my trekking boots and they tore my feet up. At the end of the day my feet were in so much pain, I wondered how the rest of the trip would go. I imagined myself on the last day with blood soaked boots, crawling up to the 17,800 foot elevation pass that we were targeting. Ok, it was a little dramatic, but that's how it played out in my head!

After that I ended up wearing hiking sandals for as much of the hiking as I could (until there was snow on the ground and the whole sandals and socks thing wasn't working out anymore) and slowly my blisters began to heal. Every day it seemed like we walked through different terrain. The first couple days we saw rivers and *huge* waterfalls like I've never seen before amidst the lush greenery.. Then we walked through apple orchards, pine forests, and arid, "wild west" style valleys until eventually getting to the snowy peaks. Along with the terrain, my body pains changed every day. One day it was my blistered feet, another day it was my hip flexers, another day my back and shoulders, and another day the arches of my feet (or lack of arches since I'm practically a duck).

The point is, when something hurt I would be tempted to think of the next nine, or eight, or three days ahead of me and wonder if it would get worse and how I would make it to the end. Instead, I focused on the steps in front of me and making it through that day. By the grace of God, the end of each day would come and most times I would wake up the next morning and the pain from the day before wasn't bothering me anymore. I was in a new terrain with new challenges.

The part of the journey you are on now might feel overwhelming. You might not be able to imagine what more God can use you for or what other challenges He might lead you into, but I can assure you, when the next step comes, there will be grace for it. You might feel at times like this is all more than you signed up for, and it is! "Exceedingly and abundantly more." God is expanding your capacity and preparing you for mountain tops. Just let Him do that, while you keep focusing on putting one foot in front of the other. One obedient step at a time.

CHAPTER THIRTEEN

Obedience's Active Ingredient: Risk

If you ever want to challenge your faith read a book called *The Heavenly Man* about Brother Yun in China. Like I did, you may think you're a good Christian, that you have laid down a lot for Jesus... but your thinking may change after you read that book. I read it when I was in a season of feeling like God was asking too much from me, only to come to the revelation that I have given NOTHING to Him compared with what He deserves.

Anyways, read the book for yourself and maybe have your own life-wrecking revelation. But I want to share one story with you. Brother Yun landed himself in prison for the third time for preaching the gospel. This time the series of events that happened at his arrest left his legs so injured he was paralyzed. The government officials were afraid he would try to escape the prison, since he had eluded their officers many times before, so they thought breaking his legs would be good insurance to keep that from happening. He didn't know what his fate would be but heard rumors that he would be held for ten to fifteen years or a life sentence. His entire time in prison was spent in solitary confinement, except when he had to be carried to the bathroom and the torture room by another imprisoned pastor. This pastor kept telling Yun, through the direction of the Holy Spirit, that he should try to escape the prison. Yun thought he was crazy because he couldn't even walk on his own!

Until one day the Lord spoke to him through scripture, through a dream, and one more time through his pastor friend. It was enough for Brother Yun to know God was telling him to escape the prison, and he acted in obedience immediately. He told the guard he had to use the bathroom, his cell was opened and his friend was let out to assist him. He put on his pants, stood up, walked out of his cell, and walked through the door to the stairway just as another believer was being brought back to his cell. He proceeded to walk through three other iron doors, normally guarded by two guards each, all standing agape with no guards in sight! He walked directly in front of another guard sitting at his desk, and past dozens of guards outside in the courtyard. It was as if everyone was looking right at him but not seeing him. He walked out of the gate of the maximum security prison, wondering all along if he was about to be shot in the back for trying to escape. The moment he was out of the gates a taxi pulled up and offered him a ride to his safety. It wasn't until he was hidden away in his friend's home that he realized he could walk again. Not only had God gotten him out of the prison, he had been healed the moment he got up to leave.

He obeyed God in a radical, risky way as soon as he got the word from God. Many of us would have asked for more confirmation to put our lives on the line like that. Maybe we would have waited for the angels to come and escort us out of the prison. I think that kind of move, if any, would have necessitated an audible-voice-of-the-Lord moment for me. But here is what Brother Yun said about that moment,

> *"I have learned that when the Lord tells us to do something there is no time for discussion or rationale, regardless of the situation we face. When we are sure God has told us to act, as I was on this occasion, blind obedience is called for. Not to obey God implies that we are wiser than him, and that*

> *we know better how to run our lives than he does." (Heavenly Man, 2002)*

I'm guilty of trying to figure out the end result before I initiate action. I will take risks...but very calculated ones. Like I said before, the bigger the risk the more clearly we expect the word from God to come. I've learned to do radical things that look dangerous but actually are safe. I've moved to other countries, but always had my funding ensured before I left. I've stood on a stage and sang or spoke, but with ample preparation. I've put my heart out to build friendships, but usually after the other person showed interest first. All these things can certainly go wrong but there's a small margin for error. Low risk.

Preparation is necessary. Making decisions with wisdom and good counsel is Biblical. But even with preparation and wisdom, there are things God may be calling us to do that are so out of our paradigm that it feels like we're putting it all on the line. The higher we go with the Lord, the more we level up with Him, the more risk is required as we obey Him. We may risk looking silly, or having our heart broken, or losing friends, or wasting time, or having a visa taken away, or even experiencing physical persecution.

Obedience wouldn't be hard if we got a map that showed us the exact effect that each step would have on our lives. Or if it came with a guarantee of safety and good results. Most times it doesn't. Most times we have to step out on a mere inkling, or a few subtle words from the Father. Obedience works hand-in-hand with faith.

Our ability to step out and take a risk to obey Him is directly correlated with our level of trust in Him. Would your Father ask you to take a risk without ensuring that it would all turn out for your good? Of course not! "And we know that for those who love God all things work together for good, for those who are called according to his purpose." (Romans 8:28)

For us it's a risk because we can't fully see or comprehend the plans God has. But for Him it's no risk, He doesn't take risks with our lives. He knows fully the outcome and when we are in full obedience to Him, the desired result will always be produced in us, regardless of what it looks like to us. We may even end up ridiculed, heartbroken, friendless, with no visa, or beaten and persecuted. But if it occurred as a result of us obeying God, then I can assure you that those things are not the end. As we lay down our lives like a seed going in the ground, we get to see the great fruit of harvest as a result. The harvest may be personal blessing, breakthroughs and freedom, new relationships, souls coming to the Kingdom of God, or maturity in Christ. I can assure you that no risk taken to obey Christ comes back fruitless.

I'm inspired by the Heavenly Man to live a life that is not dictated by persecution or fear or the law of the land, but to live a life in complete devotion to Christ alone. I fear that I will step out to do something and fail. But these are the promises that God gave me in response to my fears: "Whoever believes in Him [whoever adheres to, trusts in, and relies on Him] will not be disappointed [in his expectations]." (Romans 10:11 AMP) Other versions say that he won't be put to shame. Then in Isaiah 54 God speaks to the barren and says

> *"Enlarge the place of your tent, and let the curtains of your habitations be stretched out; DO NOT HOLD BACK; lengthen your chords and strengthen your stakes...Fear not, for you will not be ashamed; do not be confounded, for you will not be disgraced... For your Maker is your husband, the Lord of Hosts is His name..." (Isaiah 54:2, 4-5 AMP, emphasis mine)*

God may be asking you and I to stretch out the stakes of our tent. The boundaries of our comfort zone may be pounded in pretty deep and they may have been there for years while we remain fruitless or producing fruit at a limited capacity. This passage is saying that if the barren woman wants children, she better start making room for them. If we want to bring in a harvest of fruit, we better make room for it. We better start redefining the boundaries of what we will and will not do for God. Pull out the stakes that defined your limits and give Him your life, *without holding back*

Then there's the promise. Our shame will be forgotten. He won't leave us standing in a huge empty tent. He will fill it. He becomes our redeemer. Where we had lack before, He brings abundance.

The capacity to which God can use us is only limited by our willingness to be used by Him.

CHAPTER FOURTEEN

Obedience Versus Sacrifice

"To obey is better than sacrifice." (1 Samuel 15:22)

I can tell you from personal experience that to live a life in obedience to God's Word and directions is a very big sacrifice. I can't think of a single time that I obeyed God and it cost me nothing. That's just the way it goes in a world that is out of sync with God's order. To succumb and compromise is much easier than to stick it out and obey.

Every time we turn our hearts to say "yes" to one thing, we are saying "no" to something else. If we say "yes" to hanging out with a friend, we are saying "no" to alone time. If we say "yes" to pizza, we may be saying "no" to losing the next couple pounds. If we say "yes" to going to church on Sunday morning, we are saying "no" to sleeping in. We wonder why we don't have opportunities to make an impact in our lives in the way that the woman from the missionary hospital in Nepal did or that heroes of the faith like Billy Graham, or Mother Theresa, or the Apostle Paul did. But do we ever evaluate our lives to see what we are saying "yes" to? If we are saying "yes" to Facebook, Netflix, video games, and shopping throughout our day, is it any surprise that we are unknowingly saying "no" to the pursuit of our calling?

Let's take another look at my love life, or lack of it. I've watched friend after friend get married. My mom has joked with me that I'm like the girl on *27 Dresses*, always the bridesmaid and never the bride. But my mom also told me many times that God would have the perfect person picked out for me, that I have a special calling and for that I would need a special man. Of course moms have to say that kind of stuff. I had many complaining sessions with God, crying out things like, "Why do *I* have to be the one with such a specific call that it seems like no one could possibly fit into it? Why do *I* have to be held to such a high standard?" There were other seasons when I asked, "Why me?" Except during these times I wasn't asking why God had chosen to bless me, but why God had burdened me with such a calling that deprived me of so many of my desires.

My point here is that saying yes to obedience means saying no to a bunch of other things. It's inevitable. But as I hope I've been illustrating throughout this book, God has made all those sacrifices worth it.

On the other hand we can make sacrifices outside of obedience to God. We can put ourselves through hell for the sake of the Gospel, doing something that God never asked us to do. There may be fruit that comes of it for a while, but in the end our efforts will be found worthless. *The blessing comes from the obedience, not from the sacrifice.* The typical end for sacrifice made outside of obedience to God is burnout.

Often we are driven by needs that arise or opportunities that are presented. The church desperately needs people to serve in the children's ministry, so we volunteer. We get a chance to work for a great boss with great benefits so we leap at the opportunity. Our friends need a babysitter so we quickly jump in to help them out. These are all noble things that we should absolutely do, if God is asking that of us. But just imagine, you could be saying yes to sacrificing something that God isn't asking from you, and unknowingly be saying no to the fruit God has for you on the other end of obedience!

Right before I moved to Thailand I lived in my hometown for about ten months to prepare. During that time I knew I was to serve my home church however they needed me to. I approached the pastor shortly after moving back home from college and shared my heart with him. I told him that if there were any areas the church needed help to just let me know. He shared a few things that he wanted me to pray about and then he cut to what he really wanted me to do; serve in the children's ministry. I knew that I was to serve the church in whatever capacity was needed so I accepted the assignment even though children's ministry has always been far from my number one passion.

Well, eventually serving in the children's ministry turned into being the interim children's pastor while they started the search for someone long term. By the end of my time serving the church my pastor didn't want me to leave. There was a wide array of ministry jobs he was willing to offer me, although ultimately he said he knew that God was calling me to the foreign field. He knew that I wouldn't compromise moving where God was leading me so that I could stay in my hometown. God had called me to serve the church for a season, but He had other things in store for me in the next season.

This same scenario has happened to many people I know. Right as they're getting ready to launch into their season of walking in their ministry calling, another opportunity presents itself. It may be a relationship, a pay raise, another amazing ministry opportunity. But it's a distraction from the enemy, attempting to keep them from God's best for them. These opportunities may seem good, but if they aren't in God's instructions, they are a detrimental distraction.

We can waste time and money on the mission field, preaching and praying and teaching and leading and never get anywhere if we aren't in the right place. We can fight human trafficking and stand up for the rights of the afflicted, but if we are outside of God's plan then we will be fighting a powerful army in our own strength. We can sign up for every ministry at church, or work every day to feed our families, or study diligently for our master's degree. But no matter what sacrifices we make, they are futile if they aren't done in obedience.

Let's look at the context in which God gave the instruction "to obey is better than sacrifice." We find it in 1 Samuel 15. Saul was King of Israel at the time and they were at war with Amalek. God basically told Saul that he wanted to punish the Amalekites for the way they had treated Israel and that he should utterly destroy them. God commanded Saul to not leave anything or anyone alive. Saul obeyed God and ambushed the people and killed them all. Well...not *all*. In verse 9 we read,

> *"But Saul and the people spared Agag and the best of the sheep and of the oxen and of the fattened calves and the lambs, and all that was good, and would not utterly destroy them. All that was despised and worthless they devoted to destruction."*

As I read the list of all that they spared...it seems a lot more extensive than what they destroyed! They spared all the good stuff and only the things that no one wanted did they destroy.

God wasn't happy with Saul and sent Samuel the prophet to communicate that with him. When Samuel went to meet Saul, Saul was so deceived that he thought he had fully carried out the commands of the Lord! I picture the conversation going a bit like this:

Saul: "Hey Sam! Guess what, we won the victory and did everything that God said. Come celebrate!"

Samuel: "Oh really? You did all that God said?"

Saul: "Yup! To the letter!"

Samuel: "Then why do I still hear the sound of sheep baa-ing and cows moo-ing?"

Saul: "Oh those? Those are just the best ones. We decided to keep them around so that we would have something to sacrifice to God when you got here. You know, to celebrate!"

Samuel then went on to rebuke Saul for his bad leadership of the people. Because he didn't take responsibility for obeying the Lord fully, he was rejected as King of Israel.

Moral of the story, even if you are trying to do something for others or for God, your intentions are wrong if it's done outside of obedience to Him. Our works are worthless without being a part of God's plan. We're just wasting our time, money, and energy.

Even Jesus said he couldn't do anything out of his own will.

"So Jesus said to them, 'Truly, truly, I say to you, the Son can do nothing of his own accord, but only what he sees the Father doing. For whatever the Father does, that the Son does likewise.'" (John 5:19)

He had the power of God, He WAS God, and yet He didn't do anything outside of obedience.

I've heard someone say that what we start out of our own strength must be sustained by our own resources. But what is started in the will of God is sustained by His resources. We have so many things we want to do *for* God, but instead we should be striving to work *with* God. That's where the grace is.

CHAPTER FIFTEEN

Many Are Called, Few Are Chosen

I've mentioned before the night in youth group when God told me that I would be a missionary. A youth leader had come and quoted the verse from Matthew 22:14, "For many are called, but few are chosen." This statement in the Bible can be puzzling, bringing up questions of predestination and how God could only choose a select few. I'm no theologian and I can't say that I fully understand the wording of this verse, but I believe that we can find the meaning of this statement by reading the preceding story.

Jesus makes this statement after telling the *Parable of the Wedding Feast*. Basically, a king wants to throw a wedding party for his son and he invites all of their closest friends and prominent guests. However, all the guests decide that they have better things to do than to celebrate the king's son. They turn to their work instead of accepting the king's invitation. Oh, and they also killed the king's servants. Talk about rejection.

The king responds by telling his servants, "The wedding feast is ready, but those invited were not worthy. Go therefore to the main roads and invite to the wedding feast as many as you find." (Matthew 22:9) So they did just that. They brought in people from the streets to celebrate with the king's family. People of all sorts. I imagine homeless people and old women, prostitutes and businessmen. The kinds of people who wouldn't normally enter the palace, now partaking in one of the royal family's biggest celebrations.

From the rest of the parable we can assume that the people had a good 'ole time dancing the night away. Except for one man. Jesus tells us about this man whom the king caught without the wedding garments. He had his servants bind him up and throw him into the darkness where there "will be weeping and gnashing of teeth." Ouch. Seems like harsh treatment for someone who was found in the street and invited to the wedding. Maybe he simply didn't have the proper clothing for a wedding, much less a wedding in the royal palace!

Yet, when we look at Jewish culture in those days we can see that the garment that this man needed was provided upon arriving at the feast, all he had to do was put it on. It wasn't a matter of what was available to him, but rather a matter of *choice*. He showed up to the wedding but wasn't willing to go all the way and change out his own garments for the ones provided and required (Darris McNeely, 2013).

This brings us to Jesus' statement, The Passion Translation states Matthew 22:14 this way, "For everyone is invited to enter in, but few respond in excellence."

This isn't just a theological statement about the calling of God, or a point made about salvation for Gentiles. This is a challenge to our own obedience. We've been invited into the Kingdom of God through Jesus, the invitation to the Wedding Feast of Christ has been extended towards us and those who have put our faith in Jesus have accepted the invitation. We've even been offered the garments we need: garments of righteousness like the Bible mentions in Revelation 19:8. But it's up to us to put them on. It's up to us to do the *right* thing, whatever thing the Lord is asking of us.

It's not a question of being called, it's a question of being obedient.

I've started to notice a pattern when God is asking for a new, radical level of obedience from me. Usually, I start to press into Him with my questions and uncertainties, wanting Him to come and speak clearly of what He would like me to do. Most times I'm hoping that He will comfort me and confirm that I'm on the right path. All the same, I get an unsettled feeling. Then, in the midst of the unknowing, He speaks to me. Not telling me what to do in the natural, but reminding me to surrender to Him. To "just say yes" to Him. As I surrender, I have a deep, unexplainable understanding of the path that He's setting before me. This process usually involves a lot of tears. The ugly gushing kind. Because, as I've said before, surrender isn't easy.

This process happened when He called me to be a missionary. It also happened when He called me to do my internship in Thailand, when He invited me to join Go To Nations, when I surrendered my dream to go to Nepal, when I finally left Thailand, and other times along the way. Each time I received prophetic words and encouragement from other people as well as from the Word of God to "just say yes" to what God was asking of me, even though at the time I would've told you I wasn't even sure what that was. But when I let the words penetrate my heart, deciding I would say yes to Him, He made clear the path for me.

The most recent time this happened was when I was praying about a boy. A lot of things about him made sense on paper, and I definitely had feelings for him, but the timing didn't seem right and I couldn't hear the Lord speaking anything about it.

One day I was spending time with a Nepali girl a few years younger than me who has become like a younger sister. We were just talking about life and she started prophesying to me. "Shawna you are holding onto something, waiting for something to happen, but it's time for you to make a decision and act." I didn't recognize until I went home that her words were essentially the Lord reminding me, "just say yes." This led to a moment of surrender as I realized that I hadn't had peace or confirmation from Him about this relationship. I knew that I had to let it go. The Lord was inviting me to release it into His hands.

God doesn't force us to obey. He puts all the tools in our hands and gently extends His invitation for us to take part in His plans, but the "yes" is up to us. Clothing ourselves in the right garments for the assignment is up to us. The surrender is up to us. The choice is ours.

You may feel like God isn't speaking to you. Like He hasn't called you. But have you really opened up your heart to receive direction from Him? Even if it's not what you wanted it to be?

God already extended His invitation toward you. He already has your calling mapped out. The only thing remaining is to determine if you will choose it; if you are willing to lay down your own plans for your life to pick up His.

CHAPTER SIXTEEN

Obedience to Man

Maybe for you obeying God is easy. (If you think that's true then you might want to check in with Him sometime soon. There's a good chance He has something for you outside of your comfort zone... remember how we talked about the risk?) Maybe you trust the things He speaks to you, but you're not so keen on following the other people who are telling you what to do. After all, man is imperfect right? God wouldn't ask us to obey someone who's *wrong*, would He?

Yes, He would.

Before I go any farther, I just want to say, I am no expert on this subject and people much more experienced and qualified have done intensive studies about the topic of submission in the Bible. If, after reading this chapter, you sense you might need some growth in this area, please look more into it. The book that impacted me most as

I was starting to learn this lesson was *Spiritual Authority* by Watchman Nee. If you are ready to be challenged and possibly a bit offended for the sake of growth, go ahead and pick that one up.

I think there are probably three kinds of people reading this book. First, those that don't understand why they would need to obey anyone but God. Second, those who think they know how to submit but have never actually been challenged. And finally, those who have a revelation of true Biblical submission. Before I moved to Thailand, I was definitely in the second category.

I very rarely got into trouble as a child. My parents believe in a good old-fashioned spanking, but I don't remember ever being spanked as a kid. I remember a couple of times I had to sit on the stairs in "time-out" and a couple of times being sent to my room. The reason was, I just hated the guilt of being in trouble. I would cry and cry under the weight of knowing I did something wrong, something that would disappoint my parents.

When I went to a public high school, after being homeschooled my whole life, I was loved by the teachers and almost always finished my homework as soon as I got it. This behavior was brought into my youth group, church involvement, and Bible college. I kept up a good obedient facade. But in Bible College there were a lot of rules, many of which I thought were quite silly. I had my good reasons to make exceptions. I went to a concert in a forbidden venue, justifying myself because it was a Christian Artist. I came in past curfew because I was at a church event when a traveling evangelist came to town. I got a tattoo, but no one would see it, so that made it ok. And of course, other people were doing things *much worse* than me. I was still the obedient one.

In addition to my borderline actions I spoke rebellious words and had rebellious thoughts. I complained about certain departments within the school, how they were unfair and unreasonable. If I didn't like the teaching style of a professor or guest speaker, my friends and I would openly talk, not just about the points they made, but about them. We would even make jokes about some of them or skip lectures when they were speaking. I held judgements in my heart, they may have been small, but they were there all the same.

After all this I still thought I was submissive. After all, I obeyed the "important" rules. I wasn't living in any "major" sin. I never had to face major disciplinary measures or punishment. I was always polite and respectful when I spoke with leaders or professors. I sat in the second row and took notes and listened attentively as much as I could. I even prayed for school leadership. But I didn't know what standard God had set for submission.

I joined Go To Nations and stepped into my life-purpose of long-term missions like this. I had never had my will really challenged by authority, therefore I had never had the areas of rebellion in my heart exposed. Until I went to Thailand.

As I said before, I was required to do a two year apprenticeship in Thailand, during which I had a multitude of leaders I reported to for different areas of my life. I had a mentor for personal growth, outreach leaders for ministry, our team leader, the president of the foundation I worked for, and an apprenticeship director who oversaw my schedule, my training, and all these other areas combined. I had to adjust to always informing others of my whereabouts, to having decisions regarding my life discussed by at least one, usually multiple leaders, and to having very little control over my daily schedule.

On top of all of that, I was working on a primarily Filipino team. I learned that in Asian culture, the leaders and elders are usually followed without any question. They are also very highly esteemed. This might seem absurd to you or it may seem reasonable, whatever way you see it, the fact is it contrasts highly with the way we respond to leadership in America.

I remember when the King of Thailand died while I lived there. He had reigned for over 70 years and was considered a father to the Thai people, who only ever spoke words of honor and respect for him. When he died the whole country mourned. For one month everyone in the nation was highly encouraged to wear black while all festivities that would be considered celebrations were put to a halt. No music was played outside of the home and many shops even closed. Then, for one year following his death, all government employees (including teachers) were only allowed to wear black as the nation continued officially in a year of mourning.

About one month after his death it was November of 2016, when Donald Trump was elected President of the United States. We all know what kind of uproar that caused. I didn't live in the US then so I missed out on a lot of the drama, but I do know that I saw a good bit of it on social media and the news. All political views aside, I just remember being amazed that people could respond so harshly to their own nation's leader. It was the exact opposite of the honor and respect I was seeing in Thailand.

My point is the contrast in the way we view, respond to, and talk about our leaders. I don't believe that any culture is getting it 100% right, but I do know that we can learn from those who have a different perspective than us.

God doesn't just want us to mindlessly obey our leaders, but He calls us to submit to them and honor them as we obey them. Unquestionably, there will be times when our leaders make decisions that we don't like, or even decisions that are not in line with our values. In Thailand leaders began to make decisions for me that I didn't understand, and I thought I knew better. When I thought I was being stretched to my max, leadership would ask more of me. I was asked to serve in ministries that I didn't like or had no experience in. Things were administrated in ways that I found to be ineffective or unreasonable.

However, the Bible is clear that all authorities are set in place by God, whether they are beloved like the late King of Thailand, or criticized like the President of the United States.

> *"Let everyone be subject to the governing authorities, for there is no authority except that which God has established. The authorities that exist have been established by God. Consequently, whoever rebels against the authority is rebelling against what God has instituted, and those who do so will bring judgment on themselves." (Romans 13:1-2, ESV)*

I haven't found any promise in the scriptures that all authority will be fair, or good, or kind. Likewise, there's only one example in scripture where disobedience to authority was presented as acceptable. (This is found in Acts 4, when the authorities were commanding the apostles to stop preaching the Gospel, which is what God Himself had clearly commanded them to do.)

In my experience, I had no choice. I would either learn to submit or be removed from the team where I was serving. I did have a choice, however, in what my attitude would be while submitting. Would I learn to love and trust my leaders even when I didn't understand? Or would I allow pride and bitterness to keep my heart hard while suffering through doing all the things I didn't want to do?

One of our requirements as apprentices was to pioneer a new outreach as a team, completely from scratch. Up until my training, all the outreaches were in tribal villages, but my team of three prayed and we all got direction from the Lord to start a campus ministry at one of the nearby universities. It was something I was passionate about so the team chose me to lead it. For a few weeks we went to the university, prayed, worshiped, and made connections with some of the teachers and students. We started making a plan for how we would do ministry there.

The first strategy we came up with was essentially to connect with the Christians on campus, form a fellowship, and begin encouraging them while also empowering them to put on events and programs to reach their friends. Basically, we wanted to use the believers on campus as a tool to reach the unbelievers.

Well when we discussed this plan with our leaders, it got shut down. They explained to us more of the context of ministering in Thailand and why the plan wouldn't work. They also explained to us how we would need to communicate with the churches of each of the believers we would connect with in order to honor their pastors and get permission to work with their church members. They advised us to move forward in pioneering without the help of the existing believers, and then to make separate connections with them later.

I outright told my ministry leaders, "I understand what you're saying but I completely disagree with you." My mind was set so strongly on what I thought was the proper order to do things. I didn't understand that they could see something through their many years of experience in that nation that I couldn't fathom. They knew how division can so easily be created in the church. They knew that the church has the responsibility to disciple their own people. They knew that connecting with the believers would lead to another Christian club that would take a long time to reach unbelievers, if it ever did.

I wasn't happy with the conclusion but we changed our ministry plan. We began to connect with the English Department in the school and got permission to have an English Corner on campus once a week. We began to teach students, play games, and have conversations. The teachers were so happy to have us serving their school for free, and we were able to share the love of Jesus in our small group discussion times. We built relationships with Muslims, Buddhists, international students, tribal groups, homosexuals, popular kids, and outcasts. Some came to visit us at the our mission base, some went with us to a waterfall for a picnic, and some of the teachers even joined us for social activities.

We did the English Corners for three semesters, including one summer. And I loved it. But at the same time, the direction of the Foundation had changed. There was vision being cast to have outreaches in villages in the North, South, East, and West parts of our district, then later to expand to the North, South, East, and West of our province. Each team was tasked with starting one of these village outreaches, and my team of three was assigned to the South.

We went through the beginning stages of pioneering once again, this time assigning another team member to lead us. We prayed and found a location, talked to the village chief and began teaching English to Children every week. However, we didn't realize how much of a responsibility that outreach would become. We weren't just there to show up every Saturday, play some games, sing some songs, teach the alphabet, and leave. The vision was to bring the Gospel and plant a church in that village. We needed to connect to families and individuals throughout the week, host events, and disciple new believers. And God was blessing it! Within the first couple of months one of the students' father had a vision of Jesus in his room and gave his heart to the Lord. Our first disciple!

All the while we continued going to the campus and teaching English Corners where we had 15-30 students coming each week. The problem was, we didn't have time to really go deep with anyone. I was having a hard time connecting with the moms and youth in the village because of my overflowing schedule, and I also wasn't able to really invest in the lives of the students from the campus. My team members were disappointed because I didn't seem to be invested in our village outreach, while I was disappointed in them for their lack of interest in what we were doing at the university. And of course I was disappointed in myself for not really being effective in either ministry.

That's when my apprenticeship director asked me to lay down the campus ministry. I remember when she told me, I couldn't stop the tears from flowing. That ministry was my baby. I didn't understand why we all had to have a village outreach. I didn't understand why I couldn't do it all. I didn't understand why the thing that was most in line with my vision was the thing I had to give up.

Again I obeyed, even though it wasn't fun. At first my heart wasn't really in the village outreach. I just did my part every week and tried my best to follow directions from the leader (that was a whole other lesson in submission that I don't have time to tell). Externally I was obedient, but on the inside I was like a mopey teenager, not happy to do what I was doing.

Through all of these experiences, God was chiseling into my heart. Gradually re-forming me and helping me to recognize where I needed to change. In one moment of being overwhelmed I shared with my mentor, "I feel like I have no control over my life. I don't have time to do the things I want to do and there's nothing I can do to change it." Her response was to remind me that I may not have control over a lot of things in my life. I may not have had the power to choose to do what I wanted to do, but I did have control over something: my attitude. I could choose something: to submit joyfully.

Suddenly I recognized that I had chosen this. I chose to submit myself under Go To Nations and its leadership. I chose to follow God to Thailand, claiming that I would do whatever He asked of me. That was my choice and I could either resist the very people I had placed myself in submission to, or I could make my life and theirs more joyful by trusting their leadership.

It took a lot of breaking down of my own will in order for me to realize that submission to leadership is not just about being a "good person" on the outside, doing all your assignments, following the "important rules," or getting your leaders to like you. And disagreeing with leaders is not an excuse for dishonoring or disobeying them! True submission to leadership is a matter of the heart. It is honoring, even when you are unhappy. It is obeying even when you disagree. It is staying silent instead of speaking out against leaders.

Like Romans 13 says, authority is established by God. So the way we respond to them is a reflection of our hearts toward God. Sometimes we may think it's easier to obey God because He is perfect, and many times we're only in touch with the fuzzy, friendly side of Him and haven't experienced His rebuke. But people are imperfect. They get on our nerves, they say things we don't want to hear, and sometimes we openly disagree with them. We read in 1 John 4:20 that whoever says they love God but can't love their brother is a liar. I would venture to say that whoever says they are submitted to God but can't obey earthly leadership is also living an inconsistent life. We can see how much of our will is submitted to God when we are asked to submit to someone in leadership over us.

Just as our obedience to God should be more than skin deep, so should our obedience to our leaders. Our thoughts toward them should be honoring, our words about them a blessing. When they make a mistake, we cover them. When they require something of us, we follow. It's not just about us and them, our submission to them is between us and God.

> *"Obey your leaders and submit to them, for they are keeping watch over your souls, as those who will have to give an account. Let them do this with joy and not with groaning, for that would be of no advantage to you." (Hebrews 13:17, ESV)*

On a recent trek in the Himalayas, our guide kept telling us "bisthari, bisthari" meaning "slowly, slowly". We weren't very good at following his instructions. After all, we felt fine, we had energy, no reason to slow down. But he was aware of things we weren't aware of. He knew that we had to go slower so that our bodies could acclimatize to the higher elevation. He knew that our muscles would be sore and tired and that the last few days of the trek would only take us higher and get harder. He saw things we didn't.

Our leaders are in our lives for our protection and our benefit. They see more than what we see. We see our own emotions, our current circumstances, our desires. But leaders are looking at the big picture. They are seeing where we are going and how to get us, along with everything else, to the place where God wants us. If we submit to them, we are protected. If we cooperate with them, we make the journey easier.

CHAPTER SEVENTEEN

Inspiring Surrender

I went on my very first trip to Thailand in 2012. I was a senior in high school and took time out of class to go on this trip because I had wept when I saw the promotional video. I saw in the video that it was a spiritually dark place that needed Jesus, and my heart broke for those people.

My small team was assigned to do a variety of different kinds of ministry on this experimental trip but it all culminated into three nights of crusades in the city we were ministering in. Hundreds of people showed up to these outdoor meetings to hear words of hope, salvation, and healing. Many came to the front each night to receive prayer for headaches, back pain, and even deaf ears, later testifying of how God had healed them through our prayers. This was the first time I had seen miracles in such large proportions.

On the last night an older man was brought forward. He was in a wheelchair and we were told he hadn't been able to walk on his own in twenty-eight years. He was small and his legs were crooked, his hands twisted up tightly, unable to function normally for forty-eight years. Almost his entire life was spent with pain and limitations of a dysfunctional body.

As he sat in his wheelchair a couple of team members would pray for him while the others would pray for the other sick people in the crowd, then we would rotate. After some time, the Thai translator helped him to stand up as we continued to pray. Slowly, he began to walk while leaning on the translator. It was clear God was doing something, but his hands were still twisted and his steps unsteady, so we continued to pray.

Eventually someone noticed a bracelet tied tightly around his wrist. Through the translator we found out that the bracelet was connected to witchcraft and the man confessed that he himself was a witch doctor. By the time we realized this, the man had been able to slowly walk, which was more than he had been able to do in a long time. So when we asked him if we could cut off his witchcraft bracelet he consented, knowing that God was able to heal him.

I held that man's hand in mine as we cut the bracelet off of him. His fingers, so tightly crumpled, began to open and soften like a blooming flower. He closed his fist and opened it again, a simple act that we take for granted. He celebrated being able to do it for the first time in decades. God had healed him. Later that night he walked himself up the stairs to the stage and testified that Jesus had indeed healed his body.

This man was willing to give up something that he had put his trust in for so long so that he could experience the living God. He obeyed God that night but didn't know that his act of surrender would affect many others.

Over a year later I found myself in a small home in India. The family, friends of my Indian contact, had invited us over for snacks after a long day of ministry with the team. All I wanted to do was eat and then crash onto my sleeping mat under the mosquito net and sleep. But this family was opening their home to us, and as we had heard, they had begun opening their hearts to God through their Christian daughter who worked for my friend.

Our team of five Americans, our Indian friend and his wife, as well as the family who invited us over, all crowded into a small living room, sitting on two beds that doubled as couches. Their walls were plastered with pictures of Shiva, the blue-skinned god with an extra pair of arms, and other Hindu gods. They had heard the Good News once before, experienced a miracle, but hadn't made a decision to follow Jesus. This time the aunt and the father were both in need of healing. There was definitely fear and anxiety in the house. The father had broken his arm, but when he went in for surgery the doctor made a mistake in repairing it, connecting the bones in the wrong places and leaving his arm immobile.

As we sat with them the conversation naturally turned to spiritual matters. In India, religion is not a taboo topic. Talking about religion is as common as talking about the weather. It's a part of their everyday life, and there's no need to convince them that it is an important conversation. As we began to share about Jesus, who He is and what He's done, I remembered the healing of the witchdoctor in Thailand and told them the story.

They were amazed at what we told them and asked us to pray over their house before praying for their healing. It didn't take long to walk through their three room house and return to the sitting room, but during that time something happened that we didn't expect. The family began to rip the pictures of gods from the walls and dispose of them, along with other idols, jewelry devoted to witchcraft, and religious symbols throughout their home. That night they professed with their mouth and believed in their hearts that Jesus is Lord!

Later that night, the aunt called us and told us that she had no more pain and that their house felt completely different since we left, full of peace and life. On another trip we learned that the father's arm had begun to improve that day and he was even able to return to work.

This family heard the testimony of the Thai witch doctor and it encouraged them to surrender their lives to Jesus too. When people see the fruit of your obedience it will set them free to obey too. In the moment, you choose to obey because of your heart for God, but don't doubt that there will be fruit in your life that will be tangible to others. Your obedience is contagious, it will inspire and encourage those around you who see it.

A new missionary moved to Thailand about a year after I did. He shared with me one day that he had been watching me obey the Lord with joy even in hard things. He realized that he also had a choice; he could either obey begrudgingly and fight God along the way, making the whole season more difficult; or he could choose to obey God whole-heartedly.

No one wants to follow religious sacrifice that is solemn and painful and joyless. But people will follow joyful obedience. When you obey God wholeheartedly, experiencing the joy of surrender to Him and the favor that rests over your life, as a result, you *will* influence others too. Others will want to follow you as you follow Christ.

Our lives have a domino effect on those around us. We think that our decisions only affect our own path, our own destiny. But the truth is, other people are looking to us and God wants to use us in their lives. It's up to us to determine if we will lead a life of obedient surrender, sacrificial obligation, or outright rebellion.

CHAPTER EIGHTEEN

The Answer

I often have questions. I was known on my team in Thailand for being the one who asks the questions. It comes naturally. The questions aren't (always) skeptical ones. Often they are asked out of pure curiosity and a desire for things to be made clear. The right questions with the right attitude are not wrong to ask.

It's natural for questions to rise in us when God is asking for us to follow Him. It's natural to want to know how we are going to get where we're going, or when, or with whom. Especially for those of us who like to figure out the details. After all, usually when He speaks something, it looks quite impossible or at least unlikely. We can't see the hows or the whens or the whos, and sometimes we don't even understand the whys.

I've had a lot of these questions. "How do I move from here to there?" "When will I see the promise?" "Who will walk with me along the way?" "Why me?" "Why do I have to give more?" And the Father has always been gracious to meet me in them, oftentimes not answering me directly but reminding me of who He is. That He's faithful, He's never failed me, and He's got this.

Reading through the Gospels recently I've noticed Jesus calling people out on two things: lacking faith and having offense. The first time I noticed Him addressing offense was in response to John the Baptist's questions. Let me explain.

John had spent his ministry time preaching about his cousin, Jesus, and looking pretty foolish and even blasphemous to many, including the religious leaders of his day. He had been obedient to God's call, even at the cost of his own comfort and reputation. Until, for political reasons, he was arrested and imprisoned, which would eventually lead to him being beheaded, a martyr.

From prison he sent word to Jesus asking, "Are you the one who is to come, or shall we look for another?" (Luke 7:19b, ESV) I can only imagine how John felt. He gave everything to do what God asked him to do. He spent his whole life anticipating Jesus and what He would do as the Messiah. Now he's sitting in prison and nothing is going the way he anticipated it would. Even Jesus, the one he expected would overthrow the very Romans who held him captive, seemed to have failed him, not even coming to break him out of jail.

Jesus didn't really answer the question directly. Instead He replied to John by explaining what He had been working on: healing the sick, raising the dead, and preaching the good news. He wasn't overthrowing the Romans like John and many others had probably expected. This was a different kind of Kingdom that He was building. He ended His response with this statement: "And blessed is the one who is not offended by me." (Luke 7:23, ESV)

God is often working in ways that we don't understand. He doesn't usually meet our expectations in the way that we think He should. We don't understand His ways. Yet, He blesses those who remain un-offended even when they don't understand. Those that keep their hearts open to Him, even with questions unanswered.

In Romans 11:33 (ESV) it says,

"Oh, the depths of the riches and wisdom and knowledge of God! How unsearchable are his judgements and how inscrutable are his ways!"

His ways are so much higher than my ways and yours. His judgement is perfect and un-searchable. No wonder we can't understand it! No wonder we have questions! But we can take faith in the first part of the scripture, that He doesn't lack in resources for us or knowledge of our situations. His wisdom goes much deeper than we can even fathom.

His riches and wisdom and knowledge is like a deep crevice in the earth. So deep that you can't see the bottom or the walls of it, but you can imagine the vastness of it. Someone that vast, that deep, can't be fully searched out, and surely can't be scrutinized. He can only be taken into our limited capacity and trusted for His un-limitedness.

I recently read a C.S. Lewis book called *'Till We Have Faces*. In the book, the heroine battles with the seen and unseen, with faith and doubt, attempting to control love, only leading her to emptiness and hurt. I believe the entire book culminates into this conclusion: as she stands before the god that she had so many questions for, she says,

> *"I know now, Lord, why you utter no answer. You are yourself the answer. Before your face questions die away. What other answer would suffice?" ('Till We Have Faces, 1956)*

He is the answer to every question. When we see Him the hows and whys and whens and whos are insignificant. He's all that really matters.

A while after Jesus made the comment about not being offended by Him, He was riding in a boat with His disciples. He fell asleep on His travel pillow in the stern of the boat while a storm raged and the disciples freaked out. You may know the story. But if not, it's found in Mark 4:35-41. The disciples came and woke Jesus up and asked Him a question, "Teacher, do you not care that we are perishing?" They probably felt a little bit like John did when he asked his question: uncertain, confused, disappointed, afraid... Of course Jesus got up and calmed the storm like it was nothing. I can imagine everything going completely quiet while the water became still and the disciples' jaws dropped open. Then He spoke, "Why are you so afraid? Have you still no faith?" (Mark 4:40, ESV)

Of course Jesus cared about the disciples and wouldn't allow them to shipwreck. It's not in His character. His nap in the storm wasn't a question of His character or His abilities, it was a test of the disciples' faith in Him.

Jesus tested faith and responded to faith over and over again while He roamed the earth, and He's still doing it today. He allows storms to rage for a while so that our doubts and questions will rise to the surface, the areas where we need to learn faith.

I've been realizing that faith is a lot like trust, and trust is a direct correlation of how well we know someone's character. Jesus asked the disciples "have you still no faith?" Meaning, "After all the miracles you've seen, after all the time we've spent together, do you still not see who I am and what I can do?"

For example, imagine a trusted friend promises me that they have a surprise for me, then a week passes and I haven't experienced any grand surprise. I could call my friend and ask, "When exactly were you planning that surprise for me? Just want to make sure I don't miss it. Are you sure I'm going to like it? Is it going to be embarrassing? It better not be embarrassing! You didn't forget, did you?" My friend would probably be a bit annoyed, tell me to chill, and ignore my questions. However, a response that communicates more trust would be: "I know you are such a good friend, you keep your word, and I'm so excited for the moment I get to experience the surprise you have planned for me."

This should be our response to the things God has spoken over us. We may have questions, and that's ok. But He's inviting us to receive His words and hold onto them, to not be offended when we don't understand what He's doing, and to choose to trust who He says He is. When we trust and have faith, He will do incredible things.

Don't let your questions drag you down into offense or disappointment. Get in the presence of God, allow Him to remind you who He is, and your questions will fade away in the light of your faith in Him. You may not get all the answers you want. The closer you get to Him, the more you know Him, and the more you know Him, the less you will doubt Him and what He's called you to do.

CHAPTER NINETEEN

Opposition

Even when you have already set your heart to obey God's call for you, there will be opposition that will try to distract or discourage you from fulfilling what He has for you. We often surrender to God in powerful times of worship or at church camp or on a mission trip, when we feel His presence or we're pumped up with excitement. But when it wears off we often forget the things that we vowed to God during those times.

Maybe it's another promising opportunity that distracts us from choosing God's plan. Or maybe when the excitement wears off, and it turns out people aren't as supportive as you expected, you question if God has even spoken to you at all. Most of us realize that life isn't easy, but maybe you haven't learned yet that a life following Christ is even harder. Jesus Himself tells us that in this world we will have tribulation

(John 16:33), and that we should choose to take up our cross and follow Him (Matthew 16:24).

From the little things to the big things, we will face roadblocks to obeying Christ. Sometimes these hindrances are internal and sometimes they are external, the only thing we can control is how we respond to them.

One summer, while I was in college, I brought a team to Nepal. It was a small team of college students who were wild enough to trust a 20 year old to lead them across the ocean, up some mountains, and around a third world country. The opposition started with little unexpected set-backs during the planning process, and turned into more troubling issues as we tried to get the team to Nepal.

We had a friend bring us to the Houston airport early in the morning before our flight. We planned to fly to Chicago O'Hare domestically, meet up with the rest of the team that afternoon, and catch our international flight late that evening. However, when we got to the airport we were informed that our flight had just been canceled and we would not be moved to another flight. The airline refunded our cheap ticket cost and left us without a way to get to Chicago.

We all started searching the web for flights that would get us to Chicago on time for our international flight. But on the day of travel, it was tricky to find any decent flights, let alone to get all of us onto the same one. So we each just booked whatever we could, dividing up between three different flights and airlines, that would hopefully get us to Chicago in time.

Without boring you with the frustrating details, I will just tell you that it was one of those days when all the flights are messed up and every traveler is frantically trying to reach their destination. All of us were rerouted multiple times and just barely made it to O-Hare in time. I was so grateful when I got there, imagining what would happen if the team made the flight and the leader who had all the plans and contact information didn't. But when we met up with the team I noticed there were three members still missing.

We had dropped them off at their gate where they were about to board right before my travel buddy and I were rushed off to a flight they had just found for us. For all I knew, they would beat us to Chicago. But we didn't know their flight would be delayed and then re-routed and they would land in Chicago just minutes after our international flight took off on it's way to Asia.

As we boarded the plane without them, tears streamed down my face. I lost three team members before we even left the country. We were hoping that they would try and get on another flight, but we wouldn't have a way to contact them until we arrived in Nepal. We all believed they were supposed to be on this trip, so why had this happened?

Our layover was in Istanbul, Turkey where we found some floor space in the small terminal and waited for our next flight. One team member was reading a book called *Love Does* by Bob Goff and offered to read aloud to us. The chapter she was reading from was called, "Go Buy Your Books!" In that chapter Bob told the story of how he got into law school. Basically, his LSAT scores and his grades in general weren't exactly impressive enough to get into the school he had his eye on. In fact, he had already been rejected from many schools.

The fall semester was about to begin and Bob still hadn't been accepted to the school he wanted, so he decided to visit the dean's office. He went in and told the dean his story, his dreams of going to law school, ending his speech by saying, "I know you have the power to let me in, all you have to do is tell me 'go buy your books!" It didn't work.

If you can't tell yet, Goff is not someone who is easily deterred. Instead of giving up, he went and sat on a bench outside the dean's office. He sat on that bench every day, all day, for more than a week, from the time the office opened until the time all the staff went home. And every time the dean would go in and out of his office he would see Bob sitting there, and every time he passed him Bob would say, "All you have to do is tell me."

Even after classes had already begun, Bob continued to sit on the bench. Until finally, the dean strolled over to him and said, "Go buy your books."

His conclusion, and the point of the story, was this,

> *"I used to think God guided us by opening and closing doors, but now I know sometimes God wants us to kick some doors down." (Love Does, 2012)*

As we sat in the Istanbul airport this story struck me. We had just faced a closed door and it caused me to become dejected and give up, questioning if it was really God's will for the three lost members to be on our team. I so easily rerouted my plans, rather than persisting and believing and pounding on the door of impossibility.

Two days after we arrived in Nepal, we picked up the trio from the airport. They pushed through, got new tickets, and joined us for the rest of the trip. We faced many more closed doors on that trip: fear, sickness, transportation issues, and more. It was probably the most challenging trip I have ever been on, but out of it came one of my favorite testimonies of all my travels.

Just months earlier a huge earthquake had terrorized this small nation, leaving devastation, death, and poverty in its wake. Part of the purpose of our team was simply to help those affected by the earthquake however we could. Our local contacts chose a village that had been highly affected by the earthquake to do a food distribution. They had lost many homes and experienced many deaths. We ordered 20 kg bags of rice for all the families in the village and had them carried up the mountain before we hiked up behind them.

During the few hour hike I felt the Lord put Isaiah 61 on my heart. I had been asking God for a scripture for the trip and that is the one that He gave me. I honestly didn't really like it because it seemed so cliché to me, but I began to pray it and declare it as we walked. We finally arrived in the village and prepared for the families to come and pick up their rice. When they came, we offered to pray for anyone who was sick. They brought a little girl up to me, around 12 years old. They told me that she was unable to talk and that she was being tormented by demons. On that side of the world there is a much higher awareness of the spiritual realm, many who are sick visit witch doctors. That combined with the worship of false gods causes demon possession to be a common occurrence.

I began to pray and laid my hand on her forehead. As soon as I did she crumpled to the ground and started to squirm around in the dirt. We took her to a more secluded place and a few team members and I continued to pray over her. As we did she clutched at her throat and writhed in pain.

As we continued to pray for the young girl, the rest of the team prayed for other sick people in the village. People started to be healed right and left! One old man was healed of his back pain, and as one team member got out the guitar and started to sing, the man started dancing around the empty space. Pretty soon, others who were healed followed him, until everyone who was there started to dance.

We began to see some change with the young girl, and the first word out of her mouth was "Jesus." Her countenance changed and finally she stopped fighting and her body relaxed. Slowly we all got up and headed over to the healing celebration party.

I stood and watched the people who worshipped other gods, who had faced so much destruction in the past few months, who had lost brothers and children and parents, dancing to songs about Jesus. Suddenly, from the corner of my eye I saw the young girl. She pulled away from her mother and began to turn in circles with her hands waving over her head. Tears started to flow from my own eyes as I heard her shout, "Hallelujah!"

The scripture that I had been praying on the way up the mountain had been fulfilled more clearly than I could have imagined.

"The Spirit of the Sovereign Lord is on me,

because the Lord has anointed me

to proclaim good news to the poor.

He has sent me to bind up the brokenhearted,

to proclaim freedom for the captives

and release from darkness for the prisoners,

to proclaim the year of the Lord's favor

and the day of vengeance of our God,

to comfort all who mourn,

and provide for those who grieve in Zion—

to bestow on them a crown of beauty, instead of ashes,

the oil of joy, instead of mourning,

and a garment of praise, instead of a spirit of despair.

They will be called oaks of righteousness, a planting of the Lord for the display of his splendor."

(Isaiah 61:1-3, ESV)

I'm so glad that we overcame the obstacles that tried to keep us from that village. I'm grateful that our whole, complete team was up there to be a part of it.

How many of these amazing experiences are we missing because we're not willing to fight for what God has said? How often do we give up too soon and miss out on the fullness?

When you make it your goal to obey what God has for you for today, or for this year, or for your life, you will meet closed doors. Lots of them. You will run into roadblocks. You may even stand with mountains in front of you that seem impossible to move. Are you going to let a natural circumstance keep you from following through on something the God of the universe invited you to do? Or will you choose to pick yourself up and fight for what you believe?

CHAPTER TWENTY

God's Dream Come True

He whispered it to me once as I sat in church. It had nothing to do with the message being delivered that day or the songs being sung. It was a statement straight from Him that suddenly popped into my head: "You are my dream come true."

When God sees me, and when He sees you, He sees His dreams coming true. So what are His dreams? I believe we can get a picture of His dreams in Ephesians 1.

"How blessed is God! And what a blessing he is! He's the Father of our Master, Jesus Christ, and takes us to the high places of blessing in him. Long before he laid down earth's foundations, he had us in mind, had settled on us as the focus of his love, to be made whole and holy by his love. Long, long ago he decided to adopt us into his family through Jesus Christ. (What pleasure he took in planning this!)

He wanted us to enter into the celebration of his lavish gift-giving by the hand of his beloved Son.

He thought of everything, provided for everything we could possibly need, letting us in on the plans he took such delight in making. He set it all out before us in Christ, a long-range plan in which everything would be brought together and summed up in him, everything in deepest heaven, everything on planet earth.

It's in Christ that we find out who we are and what we are living for. Long before we first heard of Christ and got our hopes up, he had his eye on us, had designs on us for glorious living, part of the overall purpose he is working out in everything and everyone." (Ephesians 1:3-6, 8-12 MSG)

God was dreaming of us before He laid the earth's foundations! We were on His mind even then! I can just imagine Him sitting in the middle of the abyss thinking of me. Before there was even such a thing as light, He knew what I would look like and everything that would be inside of my heart. He knew every member of His family, all of His children, before He even created them.

David writes in Psalm 139:16 (AMP), "

Your eyes have seen my unformed substance; and in Your book were all written the days that were appointed for me, when as yet there was not one of them [even taking shape]."

Since we've been the dream on God's heart from the beginning, He has fiercely pursued each of us. His dream isn't just for us to exist, but that we would exist in fellowship with Him. So He pursues our lives in order to show us His love. He pursues us individually and specifically.

In the village in Thailand where we taught the children, there was one young grandmother that I was especially drawn to. Her name is Pi Joy (Pi being the title used to refer to people older than you). We met her on New Year's Eve and she was drunk, singing karaoke with her family on the small road in front of her house. She called us over and gave us festive hats so we could join in the celebration. She has that gift of making everyone feel like family. So we continued to spend time with her, helping her with her English, meeting the rest of her family, and eating at her house regularly.

After we spent some time getting to know her family, Pi Joy opened up to us about the various things in her life that were a burden to her. We were able to start praying for and encouraging her. When Easter weekend came around we found ourselves in her house again for another delicious Thai meal and decided to tell her about the holiday we were celebrating and its significance to us. We even showed her some clips from the Passion of the Christ movie. After showing these clips she told us, with tears welling in her eyes, that she had seen that movie before. She then began to share what she knew of the gospel with us!

Forty years prior, when Pi Joy was just a girl, around ten years old, missionaries came to her small village in the mountains of Thailand and showed the Jesus film. She told us that she remembers weeping when she saw the movie, amazed that someone would be so good and so loving that He was willing to die for her.

The Father was after Pi Joy's heart. He reached out to her tiny village just to get her attention as a young girl, and now, decades later, He had sent us to remind Pi Joy of what He did for her. He is intentional to pursue His children, and knows how to specifically reach each one.

God pursues all of the 7.6 billion people in the world this intentionally! He knows each one of us by name! And, while you and I may have been brought into fellowship with Him, becoming one of His dreams fulfilled, there's still so many of His children that He has yet to win over with His affection.

This is where He extends an invitation toward us. We aren't only one of His dreams come true, but we are also able to be someone who makes His dreams come true. Like it said in Ephesians 1:9, God let us in on His plans! He plans to bring everything together in Christ, so that both the heavens and the earth will be brought under His rule, and He wants us to be part of it. He made known to us the mystery of His will, the end of the story!

> *"After this I looked, and behold, a great multitude that no one could number, from every nation, from all tribes and peoples and languages, standing before the throne and before the Lamb, clothed in white robes, with palm branches in their hands, and crying out with a loud voice, 'Salvation belongs to our God who sits on the throne, and to the Lamb!'" (Revelation 7:9-10, ESV)*

We're still a long way from seeing the fulfillment of God's dreams. 3.14 billion people remain an unfinished dream in the heart of God, many of them haven't even been given the opportunity to hear the name of Jesus. There are still many thousands of people groups around the world who will not be represented in white robes at the throne of God because they haven't been introduced to their Father.

Make a Wish Foundation receives hundreds of millions of dollars every year to make dreams come true. Their whole mission is to make the wishes of children with critical illnesses become a reality. And tons of people have supported them in their goal, because we love to see dreams coming true.

Now, God isn't ill or weak, He could accomplish all of this without us, but instead He invites us to be a part of His dreams. He wants us to stand there in the end, looking at the multitudes of His children gathered, with just as much excitement and personal investment as He has. When we love someone, we become particularly concerned about their desires, often taking it upon ourselves to see those dreams come true. The more we fall in love with our Creator, the more we want to see His desires fulfilled (the cool thing is, He wants to see our desires fulfilled too!)

Steffany Gretzinger just released a song called "More to Me" that expresses this beautiful exchange. The bridge says, "Let me set a table for the One that I love. This is my desire. All I have is ready to fulfill Your longing. What do You desire?" (More to Me, 2020)

We know that Jesus was close to the heart of the Father, and He is the perfect example of making the Father's dreams His mission.

> *"So Jesus said to them, 'Truly, truly, I say to you, the Son can do nothing of his own accord, but only what he sees the Father doing. For whatever the Father does, that the Son does likewise.'" (John 5:19, ESV)*

Jesus never sinned right? Of course not. In Hebrews 4 verse 15 it says he "has been tempted as we are, yet without sin." But what about when he was 12 years old and went on a little trip with His parents and just decided to disappear on them? They were a day's travel outside of Jerusalem before his parents even noticed He was gone! And another three days of searching before they found Him!

My parents would have been pretty mad if I did that to them. Maybe Mary and Joseph were too, it doesn't say. But it does say that when they saw Him there, conversing with the Jewish teachers, they were astonished. Then his mom asked Him, "Son, why have you treated us so? Behold, your father and I have been searching for you in great distress." To which Jesus responded, "Why were you looking for Me? Did you not know that I must be in My Father's house?" (Luke 2:48-49) In other versions it says, "Did you not know that I must be about My Father's business?"

Even at that age, Jesus knew that His primary responsibility was to obey His Heavenly Father, even if that meant distressing His earthly parents. He was after the Father's desires, even if that meant laying down His own desires and comfort, like we saw in the Garden of Gethsemane.

Making God's dream our mission may sound like a big sacrifice, but it is the most rewarding path we can take. Because, you see, when we set our focus on God and His desires, they become our desires too! "Delight yourself in the Lord, and He will give you the desires of your heart. Commit your way to the Lord; trust in Him and He will act." (Psalm 37:4-5, ESV) When I make it my one desire to see God's dreams fulfilled, I will get the desires of my heart!

God will back us in everything we do when we are in alignment with His plans. We saw in the passage in Ephesians that He already bought and provided for everything! So when His dreams are our pursuit, we know that God will do everything to support us. As J. Hudson Taylor said, "God's work done in God's way will never lack God's supplies." In other words, "If it's God's will, it's God's bill!"

In John 14:13 AMP, Jesus promises, "And I will do whatever you ask in My name [as My representative], this I will do, so that the Father may be glorified and celebrated in the Son." The footnotes say that "acting as Jesus' representative means that the person calling on His name is in a close relationship with Him and wants what He wants."

Our part of this equation is focusing ourselves on being intimate with the Father, learning His heart, His dreams, His ways. We partner with Him in His desires and He does His part, which is responding to our prayers with His power and miracles that accomplish His will.

Many children dream of being astronauts, superheroes, or princesses, and end up "maturing" to an age where they are forced to chase more "practical" dreams. When I was a teenager I had many different dreams: to be a journalist, a doctor, a kindergarten teacher, a youth pastor, and more. But I can say that when I laid down those dreams to pick up the dreams of the Father, I was more fulfilled than I could've ever imagined. I didn't have to settle for a more practical dream, but instead I was able to live a life that I didn't even have the capacity to dream about.

Soon after God spoke to me about becoming a missionary, I went to Honduras with my church youth group. I remember sitting in the van on the way to the village for ministry and my youth pastor asked me one dream I had for the next ten years. I declared that I wanted to go to twenty countries before I turned twenty-five. I'm twenty-five now, writing my first book, pioneering in one of the most unreached nations in the world, and I visited my twenty-fifth country this year.

Country number twenty was China, two years ago. Let me just tell you, it was the hardest country to get to! The visa process was very demanding and had me traveling to different cities in the midst of my busy schedule, just to apply and pick up my visa. I almost gave up trying. But in that season I stumbled across Psalm 111:6 in The Passion translation, "He reveals mighty power and marvels to His people by handing them nations as a gift," and suddenly I remembered the desire I had expressed so many years ago on that bumpy road in Honduras. I had said yes to His invitation and followed Him wherever He called me since then, and now God wanted to fulfill my dream and give me nations as a gift.

Yes, choosing to be a representative of God's dreams is a sacrifice...at first. But once you embark on the journey with Him, you are going to experience the most fulfilling life possible, the life that He desires for you. You will experience the joy of knowing that you're not just His dream come true, but you can also be a part of seeing the dreams on the heart of God fulfilled.

Start Now

My hope for this book is that it doesn't just point you to my life and my stories, but that it nudges you to set out on your own journey of obedience with God. After all, my life is for Him and for His glory, so I hope that He is glorified as some of my deep, vulnerable moments with Him are shared with others.

Some of the things I shared may seem far fetched or un-relatable to you. They may have left you with more questions than answers. Perhaps you are thinking about how you can relate all of this to your own life. You may be wondering, like I have so many times, "How can I follow God if I don't know where He is going?"

Knowing the will of God is a much more complicated topic than can be tackled in this book, and I wouldn't be properly qualified to be the one to tackle it. But I do want to leave you with some practical tips for how you can obey God's specific instructions for your life. How, in the midst of your current circumstances, you can choose to obey Him and see His goodness manifest in your life. Your journey with God may look completely different from mine, and that's fine! The important thing is that you are listening for God's direction and following it with all your heart.

If you don't know what God is asking of you or how to start this journey of obedience, here are some tips.

1. Read the Word

Before you can know the specific will of God for your own life, you have to start with obeying the instructions of God that have been given to all believers. Start with the basics. Start by getting in the Word of God every single day, it is your life and your instruction manual. A lot of life's questions can be answered directly from the Bible.

If this isn't a normal habit for you, start with just a little bit every day. Maybe you can only handle a few verses a day, that's ok! Maybe you aren't ready to dissect the Old Testament quite yet, that's ok too! The important part is that you dig into what you read. Ask God how it applies to your life, how you can live it out in obedience to Him.

Many people want God to tell them what to do with the big areas of their lives: where to go to college, where to work, who to marry, etc. but they haven't practiced obeying Him in the simple things laid out in His word. They may want God to show them how to get a new job, but they haven't been faithful in tithing. They may want God to lead them to their spouse, but they haven't been practicing the Fruit of the Spirit.

In the Parable of the Talents in Matthew 25 Jesus illustrates the point: if you are faithful with a little, God will entrust you with more. If you obey Him in the little things, He will invite you to follow Him into bigger assignments. So a good place to start your obedience journey is reading the Word so you can know the minimum requirements that God is asking of you now.

2. Seek God

Jeremiah 29:13 (ESV) says, "You will seek me and find me, when you seek me with all your heart." When we determine to set our hearts on knowing the heart of God, we will surely meet Him. When we are desperate to hear Him speak, and we seek Him desperately, we will surely hear His directions for our lives.

We often apathetically stumble through life and blame God for His apparent lack of involvement, when really we're the ones who haven't stopped to listen for Him. We're the ones who haven't spent time in the Word. We're the ones who haven't prioritized fasting and prayer, time in the presence of God.

God is never far from us, all it takes is a little effort on our part to show that we mean business and He will show up. Start seeking Him in your everyday life and He will surely show up. Involve Him and He will be involved. He wants to be involved.

3. Start Small

Like all things in life, obeying God takes practice. We have to spend time with God, learning to hear His voice and follow what He is saying. We often bring Him the big decisions we are wrestling with but have no idea how to discern when He is answering.

Practice asking God simpler, low risk questions first. For example, which grocery store to go to, what gift to buy for your friend's birthday, what to order at a new restaurant and then DO IT! The more you obey God in the little things and see Him show up, the more faith and confidence you will have in your ability to hear Him and in His faithfulness to respond to you in all areas of your life.

I pray for you, as you read this book, to step into the fullness of God's will for your life. I hope that you will be able to discern His voice and be filled with faith as you make a choice to follow Him. And I believe that whenever you find yourself in a wilderness season, that it will be transformed into a gift of His presence as He walks with you all the days of your life.

Bibliography

Chu, J. M. (Director). (2018). *Crazy Rich Asians* [Motion picture]. United States: Warner Bros. Pictures.

Goff, B. (2014). *Love Does.* Thomas Nelson.

Hattaway, P., & Zhenying, L. (2002). *The Heavenly Man: The Remarkable True Story of Chinese Christian Brother Yun.* Monarch.

Hunard, H. (1995). *Hinds feet on high places.* Barbour Pub.

Lewis, C. S. (1956). *'Till We Have Faces.* Eerdmans Publishing.

McNeely, D. (2013, October 01). Lessons From the Parables: Matthew 22 - The Invitation to the Wedding Feast. Retrieved from https://www.ucg.org/good-news/lessons-from-the-parables-matthew-22-the-invitation-to-the-wedding-feast

Nee, W. (1972). *Spiritual authority.* Christian Fellowship.

ABOUT THE AUTHOR

Shawna Elizabeth is doing life with Jesus in Kathmandu, Nepal. She enjoys a good cup of coffee with friends, singing and song-writing, and exploring nature (especially mountains). Her heart burns for the people of the world to know Jesus, and for those who know Him to follow Him with all their hearts. She has been a missionary with Go To Nations for over 5 years and plans to continue to serve God in Asia until He calls her elsewhere.